GROWING BALLS

To Alan,
May you grow
your personal power
+ have a great life-

David Haffer

GROWING BALLS

Personal Power for Young Men

David N Hafter, MFT

This book was printed in the United States of America.

To order additional copies of this book, contact:
Xlibris Corporation
1-888-795-4274
www.Xlibris.com
Orders@Xlibris.com
34226

CONTENTS

For my son, Noah, and his buddies.

PROLOGUE

The Crash Course

This "crash course" is a quick overview of *Growing Balls*. Since we guys aren't much known for reading pop psychology books, I'll get right to the point, but you'll have to understand if this comes across as a little harsh, especially in the beginning.

Here goes: If you are twenty-five or under, you have no business even *thinking* about getting married or becoming a father. I don't care how in love you might be with "the greatest girl in the world." I'm sure she's terrific. But it doesn't matter how ready *she* feels to get married and have a baby. She may be mature enough to become a good parent now.

But you're not.

It doesn't matter how much money you have. You're not ready to get married and become a father. It doesn't matter how educated you are or how good a job you have. You may already be the boss to people twice your age, be great at what you do, make important decisions, and be admired. You're still not ready to get married, and you're absolutely not ready to be a father.

Don't take this personally. This is true of nearly all young men today, though it wasn't always the case. Early marriage and parenthood used to be the norm. People your grandparent's age and nearly every generation before them tended to get married early, or were expected to. But times have changed and the world is more complicated. As a young man today, you have many more lifestyle options than did your grandfather, maybe even your father. Today, early marriage and parenthood for most guys is, at best, risky; at worst, it's just stupid.

If you *are* considering wearing the ring and getting called "Daddy" at a young age, you may think you saw an "out" for yourself in the last paragraph: I said *nearly* instead of *all* the men your age are not ready to be husbands and fathers. Hold on; don't get excited. It's very unlikely—no matter how smart you are or what a great guy you are—that you're one of the rare exceptions, even thought they do exist. Guys in today's culture mature more slowly than in the past. It's not your fault, but it *is* the truth.

Don't think of twenty-five as some magic age of emotional maturity either. Most men are not ready to be good fathers until they are in their early thirties. Talk to men who became fathers again later in life, after a second marriage. Almost to a man they report not having had a clue what they were doing the first time around, and their marriages and kids suffered as a result.

Nonetheless, some young guys step up to the plate and get the job done very well; good for them, they have my respect. But even with that success, it doesn't mean getting married and/or having kids young was a good idea from the start. It's a maturity issue, and most men under twenty-five are simply not mature enough to be good husbands and fathers. However, this is *not* necessarily true of women under twenty-five—and therein lies the problem. Many young women (not girls, mind you) *are* ready now—emotionally as well as physically—and they're frustrated that the men their age do not act ready for the huge commitment of marriage and children.

Girls (any female under twenty-one) are rarely ready to become good mothers. Some girls feel absolutely *driven* to become mothers; they plan to do a great job with their kids (and admittedly, some will). But as a group, they are barely out of childhood themselves. A girl, thinking she is ready to be a mother and therefore focused on that goal, needs *somebody* to get her pregnant—and she might just set her sights on *you*.

There are a number of reasons why a girl feels the push to have a baby so early in life. But in the end, healthy or not, her reasons don't really matter. She has her own path to walk in life. What matters to me is that *you* not become the father. All kids deserve two parents who are mature enough for the job and ready for the sacrifices and responsibilities of parenthood. Kids who don't get mature parents suffer unnecessarily; plus, they become problems for the rest of us. We—society—get stuck taking care of those unhappy and uncared for kids. So, if enough guys like you start minding their sperm a little better, more immature girls will have a chance to grow up themselves a bit before they start having babies. That is my goal for *Growing Balls*.

Girls also have more life choices today compared to the few afforded to their mothers and women of generations past. Some girls will follow the strong urge to settle down and have kids when they first start to feel it. Despite the cultural changes from the women's movement of my generation raised in the 1960s and '70s, many cartoons, movies, magazines, and television shows *still* train little girls in a traditional mode where growing up equals becoming a mommy. Little girls are raised on stories of handsome princes coming to save their princesses from unhappy lives, whisking them off to "happily ever after." As unrealistic as that is, at least *a little* of that fantasy tends to stick with most girls. There is nothing wrong with a young woman wanting to get married and raise kids. There are *mature* men ready to join her in that lifestyle. But most likely, at your age, that's not you.

So what does a girl/woman do if she feels ready for a diamond ring and baby? What does a woman do when she hears her "biological clock ticking" if you, her boyfriend, isn't feeling the same way? Let's say this girl or woman is perfectly happy with her choice of guy—*you*—and she's ready to go. If *she* is mature, she will do one of two things: (1) back off the marriage and baby talk and let you catch up to her maturity-wise, or (2) cut you loose and find a more mature man. Those are the only choices open to what I call a *Worthwhile Woman*. For an immature girl, option no.1 is nearly impossible, and option no.2 is only part right: She'll find another immature guy like you to get her pregnant. A mature man won't want an immature girl as a partner or mother to his kids.

When you can attract a Worthwhile Woman and maintain a successful relationship with her, you can start thinking about being a husband and father.

Check out the table of contents of *Growing Balls*: Worthwhile Women, the women you want to attract, have their own chapter.

It is the *other*, less mature females we need to worry about.

Now (and this is *important*), if this frustrated and "baby ready" girl or woman is *not mature*, she may try and manipulate you into early marriage and/or parenthood. There are several ways she can do this. Here's a typical approach. She tries to make you feel like less of a man for not being ready for marriage and fatherhood. She may accuse you of being afraid *of commitment.*

This is bullshit, a desperate lie.

Okay, maybe it's a *little* true, but not in the way she means. *She* is saying that your hesitation or refusal to get married and have kids now means there is something wrong with you—something needing to be fixed. *I* say any fear of commitment you have is justified; you know better than to jump into something so important when you're not ready. Saying no to premature marriage and fatherhood is *not* a sign of a problem or a personal weakness. It is a sign of self-knowledge, personal strength, and growing maturity. Frankly, *anyone* with any smarts—even a mature man—will have some fear when thinking about entering a commitment like marriage or parenthood. That's normal.

Meanwhile, she may also call you immature as a way to embarrass you into doing what she wants. I'd like to say that this is also bullshit and a desperate lie, but I can't because . . . well . . . she's right about that too—but again, not for the right reasons. If you are younger than twenty-five, you *are* immature. That's a fact, not a put-down, even if she means it to be. Remember, this name-calling isn't about you, it's about her desire to be married and/or pregnant.

We'll talk about maturity throughout *Growing Balls*. Webster's dictionary says mature means "complete and ripe from a natural state of development." As a young man, you are neither complete nor ripe because you are still developing. Ironically, by turning down such premature commitments, you are showing signs of maturity.

When a girl (or woman) accuses you of being afraid of commitment *don't take the bait.* Because that's what it is. It's a taunt and a dare born of frustration. For some women, it's even a trick to make you *prove the opposite* by giving her what she wants—a ring and a baby. If she's *really* immature, she may skip the ring and be happy with just the baby ("Hmmm . . . I seem to be late this month."). Either way, you must see this strategy as an attack on your developing manhood. By pushing you for a commitment, she is selfishly thinking of only *her* needs. She is not thinking of you and your needs, and she is certainly not thinking about what her kids will need from a father. This is a self-serving manipulation. Don't fall for it. A Worthwhile Woman would not be pushing you like this. She would back off and let you ripen a bit (which means she really wants you), or she would move on to find a more mature guy. No pushing necessary.

If your girl threatens to leave you, let her.

I know this sounds cold. This immature girl may grow into a Worthwhile Woman someday—but she isn't one now. Don't start questioning yourself or comparing yourself to other guys who started young having kids and getting married. Let her go. You'll get over her. It may take a while and you'll question yourself (and this advice) more than once—especially when you're sad and lonely (or horny). Better to be sad and lonely (and horny) for a few weeks than to find yourself in a life-long attachment with a person who is more interested in using you than loving you. Worthwhile Women are not out to use you. You deserve someone like that, don't you?

Meanwhile, I know it's hard to give up on a girlfriend, especially one you really like. But don't worry. You'll get over her, and she might just help you out. Girls like this often do, but in a strange way. How? Simple: She finds someone else. After she realizes you're actually serious about letting her go, this girl, who two seconds ago was *so in love with you*, will start looking to find some other guy to commit himself to her—somebody "more mature"—which is actually the right idea. You thought she wanted you for you? Think again. Immature girls want guys for what we can do for them.

But don't get stuck worrying about it or getting angry and jealous. You'll probably feel those things for a while—that's normal. But then, you have to let those feelings go. You're much better off living your life on your own schedule than trying to meet someone else's. We'll talk later on about what tends to happen to guys who make that long-term mistake. Also, and this is important: If you break up with your girlfriend and she does take off after other guys right away, be careful not to fall into the anger trap and distrusting women in general. That's a big mistake. Women are *not* all alike. Assume that they are and you'll just end up with a bad, distrustful attitude toward women, and punish your next several girlfriends for no good reason. Instead, put your energy into thinking through what attracted you to this type of girl in the first place. Doing so will help you make better choices regarding girls in the future.

Meanwhile, if you're ever a guy in this situation, see it for what it really was: She didn't really want *you*. She may have thought she did but what she really wanted was a husband and a baby; she *needed* you to make her dream come true. She needed you to foot the bill for that dream, and that's a huge task nowadays.

It's not that immature girls and women don't care about their men. They do, in their own way, but they care *more* about the life they want to live than they do about the man who is going to give it to them. A Worthwhile Woman marries and has kids with a man who *shares* her dream, not one who gives in to hers to "make her happy."

If you're under twenty-five and thinking about getting married or if you're a guy having unprotected sex with women, I know you don't want to hear all this stuff. Your girl is different, right? She would never push, guilt trip, or trick you into getting married.

I hope not. Hey, I'm sure she's great and (I hope) she treats you like a king. But honestly, I don't care how sweet she is—or how hot. If she's pushing you for a commitment and you just don't feel ready—and have said so to her face—then she's bad news. This girl may just be *decades* of expensive regret wrapped in a sexy box that you're obviously welcome to open at your own risk. But don't say you weren't warned. There's countless guys my age who can only say, "Good luck, little brother."

You can't give in to the fear that she is the best (or hottest) woman you'll ever find. That's your insecurity talking. You *aren't* lucky to have her, no matter what other people may tell you. If your buddies think she's such a great catch, let them go after her. Anyhow, you were good enough to get this far with her, so she's clearly in your league and you were in hers. You'll be good enough for someone else when you *do* feel ready for a commitment.

For god's sake, don't worry about losing the amazing sex (or the promise of it) by breaking up with this dream girl of yours. Countless guys have been hooked with sex into premature relationships. *Don't think with your dick*. This is easier said than done, I know, but you can take this advice to the bank:

There's plenty of great sex in your future if you *grow some balls now* and do what you know is the right thing for yourself.

Not every girl will use the "You need to grow up!" approach. Others make a more spiritual sounding case. Watch out for that "But we have to stay together; we're soul mates . . ." line. It's bullshit too. Sure, it sounds nice and may even feel true when things are going well with the two of you, but in truth, there are *lots* of Worthwhile Women to love in this world. When you're ready to settle down, the Worthwhile Woman you pick (and who picks you) won't have to push you for a commitment—you'll *want* it, and she'll feel like your soul mate too. Really. The world is *full* of great girls who grow up to be great and Worthwhile Women . . . and they are turned on by powerful, passionate men who know how to stand up for themselves. They love Men with Balls. Unfortunately, in our culture, personal power is often confused with money and what it buys. Money and balls are two different things. Money is useful, of course, because it gives you lifestyle options. But money alone will not hold the interest of a Worthwhile Woman. She likes men with personal power. Personal power—having balls—is about who you are, not what you own.

A Worthwhile Woman sees more than your wallet when she looks at you. But she's nobody's fool. If you've got no money because you are too lazy to work for it or spend your free time getting loaded, playing video games, and blaming others for your failures, she'll see right through you and walk right past you. If she picks a man with more money than you, it won't be because she is money hungry or shallow. It will be because she is smart enough not to hitch her wagon to a loser who won't get off his ass.

A Worthwhile Woman appreciates you for the man you demonstrate yourself to be—and she is excited about helping you to be the man you can become. She will support you in developing your personal power, which is a lifelong process. It's not something you achieve easily or right away and then display on the fireplace mantle. Personal power ebbs and flows as we deal with what life brings us and as we learn from our mistakes. The right woman supports you as you navigate your way through life. Naturally, she will expect the same of you. Worthwhile Women have their own interests and their own lives to live.

But remember, when that time comes you'll have some normal fear about the commitment—only a fool wouldn't. But it won't be a sign of a problem. It will be a sign of maturity. Get the counsel of a more mature man to help you figure this one out. You'll need it.

Don't be ashamed at not being ready for a commitment. Whether you're seventeen, twenty-one, twenty-five, or thirty-two: if you're not ready, you're not ready. Hopefully, your energy is focused on productive things *other* than getting ready for being a husband and father. You are busy enough becoming a man. Good for you. In this book, we'll talk about becoming a Man with Balls. In the meantime, don't be rushed by anyone. You can't force readiness or maturity onto a person.

On the other hand, if *you* think you should be ready by now but you aren't, that's an altogether different story. *Growing Balls* tackles that issue and will help you to figure out what you need to do to grow in the ways that are important to you.

Meanwhile, if you recognize your not-yet-worthwhile girlfriend in these few pages, you know what you have to do: Get out. Get out now. Deal with the pain. Deal with the pressure of other people who tell you you're making a mistake. Talk to an older guy with some experience and a good head on his shoulders. He'll support you.

Or if you don't have the balls *to do what you know is right*, marry her. In no time you will:

1. lose your self-respect;
2. become the punch line of late-night TV talk show "ball-less husband" jokes;
3. become a human wallet;
4. spend the rest of your life wishing you had followed your gut;
5. risk resenting your kids for the intense demands they make on you;
6. forever search for ways to make it up to yourself.

Worst of all, if you sell yourself out, you will have damaged your ability to become a good father. By giving in to someone else's timetable when you knew better, you sold yourself out. That is not behavior you want to model for your kids, and as a father, you will find it is hard to teach what you don't practice.

Don't think you will be able to hide who you are from your kids. Kids are smart, right? Eventually, they *will* figure you out. By the time they're teenagers, kids see right through their parents. That's why they get on their know-it-all high horses at that age and go around criticizing everyone. They may not have all the facts and an adult's wider perspective, but they can spot hypocrisy from a mile away. Couldn't you?

Fortunately, your kids won't need you to be perfect, but they do need their parents to be honest—both with themselves and with them. Preparing for fatherhood is difficult enough for a man with some balls, with some personal power. Men who have lied to themselves and "bought the farm" (given in to their fears): these guys have lots of catching up to do in order to do a good job as a husband and father.

Now, there are many men who made this mistake and came out on top. The few exceptions to the rule end up with good, strong marriages and go on to become excellent fathers. Some have their ill-advised marriages break up and still become great fathers. As older men, these guys can be the best sources of wisdom around. I've also met some very impressive younger men who are stepping up to the plate and being great fathers. Actually, guys like this— young and old—are often among the wisest men in the village. But that wisdom was hard earned, involving sometimes years of unnecessary frustration and unhappiness—that same wisdom can be acquired far more easily. These men grew their balls all right, the hard way.

Do *you* have to learn the hard way? Marriage and fatherhood are tough enough under the best of conditions. Why put yourself behind the eight-ball from the get-go?

So, finish reading *Growing Balls* if you are interested in developing your personal power. It is a vital ingredient for any man getting ready for the challenges of marriage and fatherhood.

When will you be ready to be a husband and dad? When you have some personal power, then you're ready. Personal power comes to you when:

1. you come to know and like yourself;
2. you live by your own set of values;
3. you develop self-discipline, and because of that, skills;
4. you have patience with yourself and others;
5. you listen—so you can learn from others who have more experience than you;
6. you are willing to take chances and make mistakes in order to grow;
7. you appreciate your life and respect the lives of others.

Notice that good looks are not on the list. Personal power has nothing to do with looks. It is much more important to like yourself than to have washboard abs (although both in the same package are a plus). Don't bother to envy handsome guys. They may get a foot in the door faster than less attractive guys, but if they don't develop personal power, they will never be happy. Besides, most women past the age or maturity level of teenagers don't care *that much* about looks. They are nice to have but good looks won't carry you very far. Take a look around: There are lots of average looking guys who have *plenty* of female attention. Why? What separates the lonely guys from the rest?

Confidence. That's the key. Confidence comes from personal power and *that's* sexy. Women want their men to have confidence. Not arrogance—confidence.

Above all, you need personal power to be able to make good choices. At this stage of your life, you have lots of choices and you make important decisions all the time. You need all the help you can get.

So, that's *Growing Balls* in a nutshell (pardon the pun). This is the crash course. Do with it what you will. The rest of the book gives you some tools for taking better care of yourself when it comes to *all* your relationships: with women, friends, your family, drugs, and most of all, yourself.

If someone gave you this book, you're lucky. You've got a good friend. Maybe this person sees you heading for the wall at one hundred miles an hour and showing no signs that you have a clue. Or maybe you're making the same mistakes over and over, ignoring that inner voice trying in vain to get your attention. This person, whether your best friend or your mom, is hoping something in *Growing Balls* will make sense to you and help you get on the right track.

If you saw or heard about *Growing Balls* and bought it for yourself, excellent—you're way ahead of the game.

INTRODUCTION

I have spent the last twenty years as a family therapist, working with adults, teenagers, and kids—together and separately. I'm frustrated at seeing unhappy, unbalanced boys and young men being raised either without active fathers at all or by men who stumbled blindly into the role of father, more or less unprepared for the huge task ahead. If you can accept the notion that marriage for a man under twenty-five is usually a bad idea, how much worse is it for him to become a dad? And while some young men step up to the plate and end up doing a great job, the majority struggles as husbands and dads. All kids deserve fathers who want the job and are ready to give it their best shot. Sadly, in our society this is a tall order because despite what we hear from politicians on both sides of the aisle, the United States, taken as a whole, is not a family-friendly culture. Raising a kid, under any circumstances, is a tough job. It is time consuming and emotionally draining. It is also expensive. In our country, the financial deck is stacked against the ordinary workingman—which is a real problem for the majority of young guys who don't start their adult lives with a hefty bankroll.

Growing Balls is my attempt to prepare young men like you for what you can expect when you take on the roles of husband and father. Your girlfriends may pressure you to take the job before you are ready. You better think before you act.

You want to be a husband and father? You think you're ready? Great. Just keep this in mind: your job (you *do* have a job, don't you?)—even if you like it—will consume huge amounts of your time and energy. Relationships take work to keep healthy, so plan on time to feed your marriage or it will go down the tubes. Over half of marriages today end in divorce. And fatherhood? Even the easiest of babies and toddlers are extremely needy and require near constant attention. Your child's mother (hopefully your wife) is going to need help. Finding time for you, important as that is, takes *effort*. It's not like that when you're single, is it?

Once you take on these roles and find out how hard they are to do well, it's easy to get seduced into quick-fix solutions such as drinking or other substance use. You may hear yourself saying you need "something to take the edge off." A little of this sort of thing can help for a while, but "use" can easily slip into "abuse" if you're not careful; for some, it becomes outright addiction, often a ship-sinker for a family man.

In my normal role as a marriage and family therapist, it is unethical for me to "tell people what to do." Psychotherapy is about helping people set and achieve their own priorities and goals. Happily, my relationship with you, the reader, is as a writer, not a therapist—so I get to say what I want without worrying about breaking any rules.

Make no mistake: I have an agenda here. *Growing Balls* is about helping boys to become healthy men and is meant strictly for guys. For any girls or women reading this, know that my purpose here is to help the boys and men you love (or will love) to prepare themselves for the challenges they will face in their adult lives. Maybe you will get insights into what it is like to grow up as a male in this culture. If some of my observations about (certain types of) girls and women seem a bit harsh or unfair, keep this in mind: If the shoe doesn't fit, don't wear it.

Consider the long-range costs to children born into unhealthy relationships. I have, in twenty-plus years of experience trying to untangle these messes. So while I still have my compassion intact for all girls and boys, women and men, I also hear the occasional angry edge in my writer's voice, and I don't feel particularly apologetic for it.

Other writers, hopefully women writers, can help the girls who are clearly having their own problems making the transition into healthy women. The women's movement of the 1970s (my teenage years) drew the public's attention to real issues of gender-based prejudice and social inequality. Though there has been considerable progress in these areas for women (and therefore, society) there is still much work to do. I'm not qualified to write the companion book to *Growing Balls* for girls. That is a job for a woman writer. For just as well-meaning and dedicated opposite-sex single parents do their best to play both Mom and Dad roles for their kids, in truth, they can't. A boy or young man needs the help of a mature man who is willing to share his experience, time and energy in the goal of transitioning a child into an adult. No woman, no matter how smart, loving, and well-meaning is going to effectively lead a young man into his manhood anymore than a man can do the job for a young woman. Can she lend support to a young guy? Yes. Can she offer counsel? Yes. Can she lead him into manhood? No.

You guys with involved fathers (or other committed men in your lives) may recognize as familiar some of what you will read here. Dads do their best to pass on their knowledge and experience to their sons, but too often the lessons just don't hit home. Fortunately, they come across much differently when coming from other men. In many tribal traditions, it is a male relative or unrelated tribal elder—not the initiate's father—who ushers a boy into manhood.

Why is this? It is not about a lack of respect from son to father. Sometimes, no matter what culture you come from, it's just hard to listen to the old man. He's the guy who, every day, tries to keep you on the straight and narrow ("Do your homework and chores, brush your teeth, always remember this, never do that . . ."). After a while, his words can morph into "blah, blah, blah." On top of this, part of your growing up into manhood is separating from your parents and making your own decisions. Listening to Dad is sometimes the last thing on a guy's mind. However, if you recognize some of what you read here in *Growing Balls* from past conversations with your dad (or another caring man who spent time with you), then a nod of appreciation is due his way.

*   *   *

Power, by itself, has no morals. A gallon of gasoline can fuel an ambulance or be used to make a bomb—and a thousand things in between. It makes no difference to the gasoline how it is used, does it? Knowledge, in turn, brings you power because with knowledge comes an awareness of choices. We are in a most powerful position when we recognize our choices, and the weakest when we see no alternatives. How you use what you learn, whether from your life experiences or from books like this one, is a measure of your values. For my money, a guy with *balls is* a guy who lives with integrity. For the most part, he does the right thing because it is the right thing to do.

As a young man, you are full of power, and you know it. When you are in the Zone, as the athletes say; with your energy and strength, you can amaze everyone around you. When you harness your youthful gifts, your brains, body, and energy to your storehouse of power, mountains move. You are truly awesome. Did you know that most of the engineers in the mission control room during the Apollo moon flights in the 1960s—guys making life-and-death decisions in the glare of the world's media—were less than thirty years old? There is no end to the majesty of the powerful young man.

But you don't always use your power wisely. That is part of being young. By not thinking your actions through beforehand, you risk mistakes. Some are small and inconsequential; others are big and costly. The graveyards are full of young men who rushed headfirst into a big, risky decision only to have it blow up in their faces.

Maturity, a necessary asset for a father, comes from experience and learning from your mistakes. Wisdom comes from learning from *other people's mistakes*. As a young man, you haven't had the chance to gain the experience necessary to make smart choices.

This is why you are not ready to be a husband or a father right now.
When you have finished *Growing Balls*, you will know the signs of readiness.

*   *   *

For teenaged readers:
As you have just read, this book is dedicated to examining the decisions a man makes regarding marriage, fatherhood, and growing into manhood—a process I call *Growing Balls*. Right now, you're probably more interested in just being with girls, sexually and otherwise, and that makes sense. It's way too early for you to be worrying about anything else. Hopefully, you are not out there having unprotected sex with girls and risking making unwanted babies—but if you're not, I'll bet you know guys who are.

One thing you *can* think about now is the kind of relationships you are having with girls. How is it going? What is the balance of power? Do you feel weak or strong when it comes to girls and relationships? Do you say what you want or go along with whatever she wants? Do you catch yourself saying, "I don't care where we go. Where do *you* want to go? I'll do whatever *you* want to do." If so, you're already in trouble. You are giving up your power to the girl, and chances are, she doesn't even want it. Trust me, she's already on the way to being bored with you. You're losing her respect.

I am not saying you should make all the decisions. When it comes to dating, it's best to take turns in deciding what to do. But you need to have opinions and preferences. Don't be afraid to say what you want. Have some balls. This cuts both ways: If a girl gives all her power to you, you'll get bored with her too. However, don't believe the myth that you "have to treat girls like shit" in order to hold their interest. That's a gross exaggeration. You just have to have some balls, some confidence.

If you don't have a man in your life showing you how to be a man (or if you can't listen to the one who is trying to), then this book should be useful for you. It might help you to make good decisions now and in the future, the kind that keep you out of trouble and give you the most freedom in these great, youthful years, which believe me, end way too soon. The marriage and fatherhood stuff in here will be interesting. You might want to read it again later, when those issues become more present. You can talk to your dad or to other men you trust about it, see if they agree or disagree with what is written here.

In the meantime, you can use this book to start to develop what I call *personal power*. You're going to need it as you grow older; you'll find that some girls will be very attracted to you as you develop it. But don't put too much pressure on yourself regarding girls and sex. Don't be in a rush. Rushing is the genesis of many a bad decision. If you take your time, you have the benefit of weighing out your options. This is an advantage a mature man has over an impulsive and impatient one.

Remember that power is just that: power. It doesn't care what you do with it, but you have to live with the results of your decisions. I want you to recognize that you have lots of options available to you—many more than my friends and I understood when we were growing up. In a series of recent conversations about women and relationships with my adult friends, I started them off by saying, "If we only knew then what we know now . . ." We then talked about the girls we knew "back in the day."

Our impossible fantasies revolved around going back in time, armed with the benefits of our experience and the confidence it would bring us. We know now that confidence attracts girls. Not only did we *not* understand this when we were teenagers, most of us had little confidence back then anyway. If only we had a time machine. Oh my, the fun we would have. Or so we wanted to believe.

As much as my friends and I enjoyed fantasizing about being teenagers with a mature man's personal power, we finally admitted knowing that even if this fantasy could come true, we would still be ourselves. With a few exceptions, a person's basic character does not change much as he grows up. Behaviors may change and people do mature, but essentially, by the time you are in your late teens to early twenties, you are pretty much the kind of guy that you will be as a man. Your values follow you. In my if-I-only-knew-then-what-I-know-now fantasies, I am Mr. Teenage Sex God, beating my chest like Tarzan and jumping from one girl's bed to the next. But that was never in my character. I went out with one girl at a time. That's who and how I am in relationships with women. However, as a young man I let myself get stuck in some really bad relationships because I didn't have the balls to get out—and *I knew better*. So I missed out on being with some really *great* girls. Man, I'd like to go back and change that.

I feel a headache coming on . . .

Maybe something in this book will help you avoid sharing my regrets when you are in your forties. Read it and learn how to build your personal power. Then, decide what you are going to do with it. Will you abuse it by taking advantage of the girls you attract? Or will you build on it, learning from your successes and failures and gaining experience from getting to know a variety of girls and women before making a choice to commit yourself to one of them? (Choose the second option . . .)

Of all the lessons a man must learn, the first is figuring out whom to trust. We all make mistakes by trusting the wrong people. Unbalanced but powerful people are good at getting other less-confident people to trust them. Part of growing up successfully is learning how to spot the bad advice, and avoiding the loud but unbalanced guys who give it. One way to separate the weird from the wise is to look for familiarity in what they say. Wise people remind you of what you deep down already know to be true but maybe don't really want to hear. I hope to earn your trust by reminding you of the wise things other people have tried to teach you.

Unfortunately, nothing you read in this book is going to give you any experience. Nonetheless, you *can* learn from books. Use my friends and me here; learn what you can from our experiences to help you make good decisions. The lessons from many lively conversations are imbedded throughout this book. Remember, you don't *have* to jump off a cliff in order to learn the rules of gravity.

CHAPTER ONE

Your Balls and How to Find Them

For men, balls are a sensitive topic. They hang out there, vulnerable, and they're hard to protect. Your brain gets a nice thick skull as a shield, but not your balls. The family jewels have to rely on that pampered brain to come up with ideas on how to keep them happy and safe. To get hit or kicked in the balls is a shock to your whole system—that's pain you can't just shake off. For several minutes, you're doubled up and groaning. Every boy figures out quickly to protect his balls.

So what does it mean to say a guy "has balls"? Of course he has balls. *Every* guy has balls, right? Sure, but we're not talking about testicles; we're talking about balls. You get known for having balls by how you act, especially under pressure. When the chips are down, a guy who has balls does the right thing *because it's the right thing to do*. The element of pressure is important here. It implies danger, maybe even sacrifice. Your balls are hanging out there, unprotected, and you do the right thing anyway. That's having balls. A "stand up" guy has balls. You can rely on him; he has your back, so long as you are in the right. A guy with balls isn't going to fight for a thief or a fool. But don't call him a hero because he isn't. A guy with balls either has it in his character to do the right thing or he develops that value—and hence his balls—from life experience.

A guy with balls has integrity. He's not looking for a reward; he does the right thing because he just couldn't stand himself living any other way. He *acts* on his personal values. And the odds are, a guy with balls has taken some shots in his life. He has learned a few lessons the hard way; sticking to his values has cost jobs, friendships, lovers—that's the price you sometimes pay for a clear conscience. Do you see why most young men—inexperienced men—are not ready to be husbands or fathers? Being a good husband or father takes balls. Finding them is one thing but keeping them—paying the price for sticking with your values—this takes courage and integrity, and experience.

Young men like you, even boys, show some balls in their behaviors now and then—and you deserve credit when you do. Look back at some of your prouder moments when you have done the right thing because it was the right thing to do, especially when looking the other way would be easy. Maybe you have acted with courage and integrity many times. But just being young pretty much guarantees you are going to cut some corners and try to get away with some stupid stuff. Young men make bad decisions and end up embarrassing themselves. Every young man does this and every man has his stories, though he may not be in any hurry to tell them. We get caught being a show off or a braggart, and it stings to even remember it. We sell out our values for the quick score. We take silly chances with the law. We get stupid behind the wheel and put our safety, and that of others, at risk. These are common behaviors for young single men, but *way out of line* for the husband or father. Most men have to figure this out the hard way because we tend to ignore the advice of more experienced men who have gone before us.

For young men, identifying personal values and figuring out how to live by them is the main task of our teen years and right on through most of our twenties. This may sound like a long process, and it is, but it is also normal. These years of gaining life experience is how a guy matures. No one is born mature.

In the meantime, every boy deserves his time to be a boy, not a man, while he is young. But there are plenty of boys who don't get that chance. They make themselves act like grown-ups before their time. There are two possible reasons for this: the first has to do with circumstances beyond his control. Poverty or the early loss of his father will sometimes push a boy into early manhood. This is sad, and I tip my hat to a guy like this. His sacrifice must be appreciated, because like the rest of us, he is only young once. Batting in the big leagues when you belong in Little League takes balls for sure.

The second reason for an early flight into manhood, although common, is absolutely avoidable. It begins with a boy or young man's mistaken idea that he is *supposed* to be ready for a man's responsibilities when he is not. This is the guy who gets himself trapped into too-early commitments, most notably marriage and/or fatherhood. He thinks he is going to earn big brass balls by taking on the man's job, or at the least, wearing the label of husband or father. In truth, he is pretending to be someone he is not ready to be. If he's doing this to make his girlfriend happy, he's going to find that this "hero" role gets old fast.

This guy needs to check for his balls because if he had any before they're likely to be gone soon. He is in for a tough road and so is his girl/woman. If he manages to hang in there and more or less behave himself in the relationship, he becomes a prime candidate for a midlife crisis later on when he'll either:

1. try and recapture some of the fun he gave up as a too-young father, or
2. find himself depressed.

Ask any man you respect about this. He'll know guys who took the plunge too early and paid for it dearly. Even the guys who were *not* giving in to pressure from girlfriends—the ones who convinced themselves that early commitment is the ticket to manhood—usually found out too late how wrong they were. The healthy ones learn to move on without regret, taking it as a life lesson learned the hard way. The other guys get bitter or depressed.

Trust me on this: It is hard enough for the average guy who *did* have some irresponsible fun as a young man to accept the limitations and responsibilities of middle age. For a guy who sacrificed his youth—even willingly—to play the role of the mature man, the hit of middle age is harder. He may feel the urge to do all sorts of irresponsible things, from the dangerous to the silly. He may cheat on his wife, gamble irresponsibly or spend money on things he can't afford (typically, an expensive sports car), or risk his life jumping out of an airplane. All he knows is that he doesn't want to die without having ever lived—whatever that means to him.

Some of these behaviors are pretty harmless, while others can turn a guy's life and family upside down. Doing the right thing for the right reasons and acting mature day after day, year after year, is tough. Mature men struggle with this, let alone boys who take on a man's responsibilities. As he gets older and his youth leaves him, this guy's temptation to cut loose a little while the body still has some tone to it is so common that most people don't even raise an eyebrow when they hear about a middle-aged man suddenly doing weird and wild things. Frankly, even mature guys who waited to get married and found Worthwhile Women to marry go through midlife crises. Their partners understand and deal with this life event.

Less mature (not yet Worthwhile) women and girls who nonetheless feel ready to become mothers, lean on their boyfriends to accommodate them. However, if they could look into the future, they would think twice before pushing their boyfriends into premature commitments of marriage and fatherhood. The least mature among them give their boyfriends the impression that a real man proves he is one by making the big commitment. And too many of us believe it and take the bait.

Young men, take note: Learn the lessons of those guys who came before you. Don't rush into manhood. Good men are like good wines: they mature naturally, over time. You can't rush the process. There is a natural rhythm to growing up and maturing but it's not always obvious, not to guys, and especially not to their girlfriends. You have to pay attention to catch on to it, or have a wise man around to guide you.

As boys in the process of becoming men, we get off track when we try to meet someone else's time schedule. To please their girlfriends (and/or out of fear of losing them to someone else), guys get engaged and married before they have given themselves a chance to gain some experience in the world. By the time they wake up and realize what they have done to themselves, it's too late to turn back.

This "selling out" to other people's timetable or expectations happens with other people too, especially parents. Some guys take jobs they don't want because their parents expect them to or spend years in school preparing for a career that does not interest them. But they do it anyway because they want to please those who expect it of them. Usually, they're afraid to speak up and tell the truth about what they want for themselves. Maybe it is a completely different career. Maybe they want to be a little irresponsible for a while, be a ski bum for a year or two or work in a video store just because they like movies and don't feel ready to pursue something more challenging.

It *does* take balls to put your unmet needs ahead of other people's expectations. Even if your plan looks a little silly or irresponsible, it's still *your plan*. How are you supposed to mature if you never learn from experience? And if your path turns out to be a dud, so what? You'll find another one. Besides which, life is full of surprises. Who knows what you'll learn from one day to the next? In the meantime, finding the *faith in yourself* to follow your unpopular path may be its own reward.

True, maybe doing what you want to do comes off looking selfish or immature. Again: So what? By definition, a young man *is* immature. Young is the *opposite* of mature. Don't worry about being immature, and certainly, don't take it as an insult when someone calls you immature. This can be hard because it feels like an insult (and is usually meant as one). But it's really just a fact. So what? You can choose to let the insult pass you by. Don't take the bait.

"Of course I'm immature," you might say. "I'm young. What's your point?"

You're right on track for who you are and where you came from. You'll mature according to your own schedule. Remember whose life we're talking about here.

Is it your job, as young man, to make other people happy, especially at the cost of your own satisfaction? Please answer no, because if you say yes, get ready for a ton of serious compromising. Because when a boy puts on the coat of a mature man, he compromises himself by giving up his youth. Are you ready for that? It's buying a house from a pretty picture in the newspaper without ever stepping foot inside, getting the inspections done, learning the purchase price or the monthly mortgage payments. That isn't having balls, that's being stupid.

CHAPTER TWO

Taking the Plunge and Conscious Compromising

Here's the truth: When it comes to being a husband and father, if you're going to do the job right, you have to be conscious of the compromises you are making and are going to make. You have to make peace with those compromises or you'll either drop the ball, letting your family down; or you'll be resentful as you grudgingly fulfill your responsibilities—or both.

Don't believe me? Ask some men you know and trust about this. They all know guys who blindly took on the job, or may even be one. Guys who have made commitments without considering the compromises they will have to make are hardly ever in a good mood (unless they're loaded). They tend to come across like life owes them something that they never seem to get. It rarely occurs to this type of guy that he made this mess for himself. So, if you're ready to be a husband and a dad, the answer to the question, "Are you ready for that much compromise?" had better be yes. Don't get me wrong. I'm all for you becoming a husband and father if that's what you want and when the time is right. There are great joys in those two wonderful roles; moreover, the necessary compromises to do them well are perfectly okay—but only for the man who knows what he is doing and is ready for the job. His compromises are conscious ones.

As a husband (or even a serious boyfriend), you are suddenly in a *partnership*—and partnerships always include compromise. Hopefully, you will have partnered up with a Worthwhile Woman who understands that the relationship means compromises for her too, because partnerships are fifty-fifty deals. To build a good relationship, the couple looks at one another's needs and desires and puts plans together on how to get as many of those needs met as is reasonable and possible. This means setting priorities you both can live with. Both people have to be happy with the deal or the relationship will break up, as so many (almost 60 percent) do. I'll let you in on another little known fact: Relationship agreements have to be *renegotiated* every so often. Why? Because people and their life circumstances change over time. That's why so many couples break up after many successful years of marriage. When changes come, the marriage needs to be able to roll with them. When the changes require more compromising than one of the people can tolerate, the marriage ends. Up until that point, everything is negotiable. You and your Worthwhile Woman have to get good at negotiating compromises that work for you both.

As an unattached young man, you don't *have* to factor in the expectations of a partner. Instead, you get to focus on experiencing life, which, as we have identified, is how you mature. Young people deserve time to try new things, take chances, make mistakes and figure out their values—not just the ones they were taught, but the ones you come to own from your own experiences. That helps you grow your balls.

There is no one set formula for how to be a good husband and father, although balls are required for both jobs if either is to be done well. In terms of being a husband, there are as many ways of being a good husband as there are types of marriages; not all wives have the same expectations of their husbands. A good match between people is one where mutual needs and expectations are clear and agreed upon.

But get this: When a guy *doesn't even know* what is really important to him, he can't enter into the relationship with any clarity. Even if he has some integrity and courage—in other words, some *balls*—he doesn't know what to do with them. Where does he make his stand? What can he tolerate? What is off limits and beyond compromise? You have to think these things through before you commit yourself to a woman *or she'll make those decisions for you.*

Feeling pushed into a compromise almost always breeds resentment. Take this simple situation: Plans for Saturday night. It's natural for a committed or married couple to check in with one another before making plans for Saturday night. Couples usually have an on-going trade off of some sort unless they like exactly the same things. Hopefully, the compromises feel fair for both people. On the other hand, if your partner expects you to give up *ever* going out with your buddies on a Saturday night, that's a compromise you're free to agree to, but I certainly wouldn't. There's no rule saying a good husband has to accept unreasonable terms. Most likely, a woman like this won't outright *say* you can never go out. She'll just give you trouble every time you try.

Being a father is *way more intense* than just being a husband—which is why most guys need time to adjust to being a husband before they take on the role of dad. Rushing headfirst into a pregnancy right after marriage is a mistake for a young couple because it puts so much extra pressure on the new marriage. This makes getting married because of an accidental (or careless) pregnancy a terrible idea. Unless both partners really want to jump right into parenthood, it is best to have some time together as a couple before making babies. Eventually, the kids will grow up and leave you alone again; you'll be the couple you were before having kids. It's best to have some identity as a couple to fall back on. Many such couples are lost when their kids grow up and leave.

As a father, you give up far more of your autonomy than when you became a husband, and that's normal—it's just part of the job. Raising kids has tremendous rewards and it's been called the most important job you will ever have, but doing the job right means making regular and significant sacrifices of your time, money, and energy. You are kidding yourself if you think that isn't true. Talk to some dads who seem to be doing a good job. They'll tell you. So, as important as it is for a father to give himself some alone time *and* play time with his buddies, pulling it off takes effort and planning. Why? Everyday life keeps you plenty busy. At least some of what little extra time you do have goes to your kids. Why? Because kids *deserve* their dad's time and attention. They really need it. If you're not ready to give it to them, you're not ready to be a dad.

Both parents need breaks from kids in order to be sane and good to themselves. You can't expect your wife to be attentive to the marriage if she has no energy left at the end of the day. Again, here's where compromise comes into the picture. Depending on whether both people have outside jobs or not, daily issues like housework, cooking, paying the bills, and so on require planning if they're going to go smoothly. A healthy couple figures out the problem but it *is* hard even under the best of circumstances; there will be times when outside pressures make the daily chores seem almost impossible to accomplish.

Without dragging this out, let me just say this: it's nearly *impossible* to describe to you, a young man, just how hard and tiring a job parenting really is. These young girls who say, "I don't care what *anyone* says: I *can't wait* to have a baby!" are *nuts*. They're so caught up in their mommy fantasies—they so *need* a baby to love and love them back—that they can't think straight. Even when people try to warn them, they don't listen. They'll never believe the hard truth of parenting until they figure it out for themselves; at which point, they either buckle down and do a good job or they pawn off their responsibilities on other people. That's why so many grandparents are getting stuck raising their grandchildren.

When your girl is absolutely convinced she is ready for a baby, she needs *you* to be ready too. We'll spend a lot of time in this book helping you figure out when you are ready to be a husband and a dad. That's not a decision you want to be made for you.

When you get there, read the Worthwhile Women chapter carefully. You need to know how to spot a Worthwhile Woman, or a girl on her way to becoming one. If you don't, you risk hooking up with her immature opposite and all the headaches her type brings. This also puts you at risk of falling into fatherhood before you're ready. If this happens to you, blame yourself, not her. These were your decisions. You either didn't have the balls to make the right decisions (including making sure you used *reliable birth control* every time you had sex), or you didn't listen to the warnings to slow down.

I understand the strong desire to make your girlfriend happy; I also agree that a woman who feels ready for commitment can be *very* persuasive. In her frustration over your resistance, she may point out other guys you know who have taken the plunge, and measure you up to them. In response, you'll be tempted to rise to the challenge and prove you can be just as big a man as these other guys. Even some of your married buddies may try and convince you to "join the club" and accept your fate the way they accepted theirs.

This nonsense makes the hair stand up on the back of my neck. Your manhood is being attacked. Don't accept *anyone's* judgment on you. If you're honest with yourself, you'll know when the time is right to make that sort of commitment. If you're not sure, don't do it. Find a mature man to talk with before signing on the dotted line.

You can't feel bad about saying no. For young men, saying no to too-early commitments is an *excellent* way of finding and keeping your balls. You are recognizing your own immaturity—which only means that you are not ready. You have nothing to be ashamed of in admitting that you are not ready for a relationship commitment. The shame would be in giving in when you know better. In saying no, you have thought the issue through and made a decision. Right or wrong, you're sticking with it until you feel ready for the life changes you know are coming.

So, let's say you respond beautifully to pressure for a commitment. You say "No, not now." Period. What is the cost? What will you give up? If she cuts you off from sex until you agree to send your boys upstream, then she's doing you a *huge* favor. She's giving you a taste of your future. This is a wake-up call. Don't be blackmailed. She has no real power over you. Thank her sincerely and then break up. Don't worry about being lonely. You found her; you'll find someone else.

Afraid she'll find someone else? I promise you, she will. So prepare yourself to deal with it. Get your ego out of your way. Because when she runs off and finds someone who *will* give her a ring and a baby, you'll realize that she wanted those things more than she wanted you.

This is a brutal truth. For her baby's sake, you should hope she found a man who *is* ready to be a husband and father. Otherwise, the kid will be raised by a guy who sacrificed his balls to make her happy or just to get laid. That rarely works out well.

However, I admit that this sort of thing is hard to watch. It is easy to second-guess yourself when you watch some other guy marrying your old girlfriend. The answer is to trust your decision. Focus on building your skills, working towards your dreams, and generally making yourself proud in all that you do. Do that and you're *guaranteed* to grow some excellent balls and do a good job of keeping them.

CHAPTER THREE

Confusing Heart with Balls

(and Other Tales of False Balls)

It is easy to confuse having balls with having heart. Great athletes have heart. Some have balls too, but if they do it has nothing to do with what they do during the game. Giving the famous "110 percent" on the playing field is playing with heart—which is great and admirable. But it's still *play*. No matter how tough the game, it's still a game. It is entertainment and theater; more of an "as if this is really important" than a real-life circumstance where guys with balls are made and live. To be a great athlete, you have to believe—during the game—as if it really matters who wins and who loses when it really doesn't. I like sports too, but let's be serious: sports aren't life and death situations. We say it takes "balls" to do all sort of things requiring some courage: diving into a river, trying stand-up comedy, or some other stage activity where public embarrassment is a distinct possibility. I can respect those efforts. Let's say they take some guts to do, but for the sake of clarity, if not argument, let's reserve having "Balls" for riskier and more selfless behaviors.

Soldiers have balls. Cops have balls. Firefighters and members of rescue crews: these people definitely have balls. They live with their fears and still do their jobs. But these are not the only people with balls.

Most of us are not called upon to go into battle. We don't get the 911 calls and face the ugly or dangerous side of life. Unless you're a cop or a soldier, you're not expected to go head-to-head with the bad guys. With only rare and unplanned exceptions, it is the trained firefighters who charge into burning houses and buildings—not the rest of us. Smokejumpers parachute into raging forest fires and attempt to stop them before they threaten the rest of us. Of course, that lifestyle is their choice and clearly not for everyone, but we're all damn lucky there are men and women willing to take those jobs. Meanwhile, *all* men need their balls, but all men aren't going to be cops, soldiers, or firefighters.

So then, how about the rest of us? How do we grow and keep our balls? A guy with an average type of job might someday find himself in a potentially heroic situation, facing unexpected danger of some kind. He will need his balls to be brave. Most of us, however, find we grow and keep our balls by living with **integrity**: being honest to ourselves and others, living according to our principles (which require us knowing what our principles are to begin with), walking the walk, and doing the right thing because it is the right thing to do. We live with integrity by *demonstrating* our morals and values.

My ideas about having balls are not shared by all men. Bad Boy types certainly believe that *they* have balls (and Nice Guys don't—and never will). They tell their sons to act like "men" when they are still young boys, thinking this is the way to grow balls. This is a bad strategy because a boy has no idea what it means to act like a man. How *is* a boy supposed to act like, let alone be, a man? Many guys in their early twenties, let alone kids or teenagers, are not ready to be men. But you still hear men harping on their eight-, ten-, or twelve-year-old sons to act like men. Fathers tell their young sons to "take care of the family" while they're gone on business trips. It's a nice thought, I guess, but what does it really mean? Even at this age, I have no idea and neither do the boys given this heavy-sounding directive.

Boys are busy trying to find some personal identity while still needing to fit in with the crowd. They aren't emotionally ready or mature enough to, as the saying goes, "march to their own drummer." They may act tough, but usually only in groups (including gangs) where they have a support group of like-minded guys. Most guys find their own kind to hang out with: brains, stoners, jocks, musicians, gang members—all different types. They hang together for a sense of belonging. This is all normal behavior. For the most part, guys who don't fit this description lack the skills or confidence to seek out and maintain friendships. Boys are not ready to go against their crowd—not usually.

To be a man with balls, you have to be ready to do the right thing because it is the right thing to do instead of "following the crowd." A man with balls chooses his friends carefully. Boys usually don't; at least, not until they get some experience under their belts.

While not a man, a boy can and should begin learning how to make good moral decisions. This is how character develops and why the attentions of healthy men to teach him are so important for a boy. He can learn to act on his growing knowledge of right and wrong. He can learn to follow his gut and to resist the temptation to do the wrong thing even if he thinks he won't get caught. This takes time because he will see other kids getting away with things that look fun to do.

His father or another man who is committed to his growth can help with this. A boy can start developing his balls early on, but he'll not be able to keep them; you can only expect so much of a boy. He'll behave heroically now and then—standing up for the little guy or confessing to his own mistakes and making them right. At times like that, sure enough, he'll look down and there his balls will be. (When you become a dad, be ready to praise your kid for this. Hopefully, someone is noticing and praising you for your manly behaviors.)

But before too long (and as is typical of all boys), he'll lie his way out of a tough situation, or do something stupid, selling himself out in the process. And poof, off go the balls until the next time he does the right thing for the right reason. Hopefully, there will be a man in his life who will talk him through both types of experiences. He'll remind the boy that character development *does* begin on the playground. He'll keep the boy honest, making sure he is strong enough to not join in with cruel, stupid, or illegal behavior. But a mature man won't expect the boy to be a man. Instead, he'll point him in the direction of mature manhood and challenge him to arrive there someday.

The character you are developing comes from the behavior of the people who are raising you—your role models: parents, relatives, family friends, coaches, and teachers.

From the safe place of fitting in and being a part of his crowd, a boy—hopefully with the guidance of mature men in his life—begins figuring out what he wants for himself that might end up setting him apart from the crowd. From there, he starts to figure out the price he will have to pay to get it. For instance, the developing young athlete or musician realizes, at some point, that he'll have to start putting in the necessary practice hours to get good. Some pushing from adults in the beginning is okay. Helping him to hang in there at the start—before he feels much progress—can be hard. However, if you have to keep pushing a kid to practice his skill, he's telling you he is not ready to learn it. Even if he follows your directives to practice, it is likely he won't appreciate the skill or own it—he did because you made him. You don't get balls by being forced to do the right thing. Your best bet is to have your own creative projects. The boy learns more by watching your example than by any lecture you can give.

*   *   *

Where are all the Good Role Models?

Most kids watch too much television and play too many video games. Period. What's the problem with this? For one thing, kids are getting fat and lazy because they're not out burning calories and learning new skills with their bodies. They are not developing social skills because they're parked in front of the television or computer for hours at a time. It's a tough situation because the games and shows are *so good* at capturing kids' attention. Kids are so dazzled at what they see that they don't bother learning to be creative. Someone has been creative for them already. It takes no skill to turn on a television. Mastering video games takes skill, I admit, and there is some pride in making the next level or beating the high score. But I'm quite sure this isn't enough to build up a boy's character or self-esteem.

Boys growing up without their dad's attention miss out on who should be their number one role model. If his dad is too busy to do his parenting job, or if he's absent altogether, boys tend to turn to television for inspiration and role modeling. This is a *severe* problem when it comes to finding your balls. It is almost impossible to find a man or male character on television with balls. Let's start with cartoons, the first television most boys watch. I go **nuts** seeing men portrayed on cartoons. Most often, Cartoon Man is a weak-willed wimp. I think of the cartoon dads I grew up with, like George Jetson or Fred Flintstone. The more modern cartoon dad is Homer Simpson. These guys are always sneaking around in order to do what they want to do because they're **too scared to stand up for themselves.** They're also usually fat and sloppy in their appearance, a sign that they have little discipline or self-respect. Their wives constantly nag them and they reply like wimps: "Yes, dear," they say. "All right, Dear. Right away, Dear . . ." Blech . . . You won't find any good role modeling there. Not a set of balls in sight. Why is Cartoon Man so scared of his own wife? It's no wonder guys grow up hesitant to get married.

Cartoon Man has other problems too. His boss constantly abuses him by treating him disrespectfully. He gets fired for making a mistake or for daring to stand up for himself. How's *that* for a couple of messages to instill in little boys? Don't dare admit your mistakes or you'll get canned. Stand up for yourself and show some balls—and you'll get them cut off and handed right back to you.

Cartoon Man is portrayed as an idiot and a buffoon, leaving you to wonder if he really *deserves* to be treated any better. He lives his life scared to death and powerless. The only way to get power, according to the cartoons, is to *become* the boss. When this happens, inevitably, the new boss becomes just as big an asshole as the guy he replaced. And why not? What kind of role model does he have? Have you *ever* seen a good boss portrayed on a cartoon? They are all power freaks. So what message are we giving to our kids? Power leads to abuse. Get power and then abuse it or you will be abused by others in power. Doesn't that sound fun? No wonder kids are afraid to grow up. No wonder guys in their twenties are still stuck in front of their televisions, joysticks in hand, playing the hero role in video games instead of life itself.

Meanwhile, does power have to corrupt? There are plenty of examples where it does, but it doesn't have to. Can't a mature man be a boss? Of course, but in the real world, we don't hear much about them. Now and again you hear about a mature boss who runs his or her company fairly and treats their employees with dignity and respect. And we're amazed . . .

Do men have to be weak and pathetic to be funny? Why can't a man with balls be funny? Does he have to melt and fall apart at the sight of a beautiful woman? If Cartoon Man isn't caught brain dead, babbling and drooling at the sight of a babe, he is foolishly falling instantly "in love." His heart bulges out of his chest, his knees go weak, and he's left bent over double with his eyes bulging out over his big belly and slobbering tongue. He's totally out of control. The women in the cartoon (and all the little girls watching in television land) see Cartoon Man as foolish, weak, and easy to manipulate. He is not to be taken seriously. He's a *doofus*. Cartoon Man, like a child, pretends to be better than he is. He has no real self-esteem so he can never really be proud of himself. His wife (correctly) sees him as a big child, not a man—and treats him that way.

Man, I'm tired of this guy.

This was your television role model: Cartoon Man, who spends so much time entertaining us boys when we are young and impressionable, *has no balls*. Why are we preparing generation after generation of boys to live a powerless existence? Why do we men put up with this bullshit?

For Cartoon Man to behave like an actual man (with balls), he has to be a *Superhero*. Superheroes do the right thing because it is the right thing to do. They have balls, but it takes superpowers to get them. They keep their dignity around beautiful women and face danger willingly and without fear. Well sure, with superpowers, who wouldn't? Nonetheless, we boys learn about heroism from these super-characters.

Cartoon Man very rarely shows any personal strength. When he does, it is usually by accident—something simple he does gets interpreted, wrongly, as being heroic. And rather than 'fess up to the mistake, Cartoon Man takes the credit as he is celebrated as a hero. The message? Regular guys are never real heroes and certainly do not have balls. They may stumble upon their balls now and again, for a little while, but they can't hold on to them. There seems to be no kind of real man in between Cartoon Man and the superhero. Sure, the superhero is going to be brave. He has all those cool powers. He can *afford* to be brave. Unless the bad guy has a pocketful of kryptonite, Superman is at no risk going after him.

I wish this stupid portrayal of men stopped at cartoons. But it doesn't. Situation comedies are full of men with no more balls than Cartoon Man. Dad is usually the lovable idiot, a slave and victim to huge monthly bills, a job he hates, kids who don't respect him, and a wife who is usually disappointed in him.

By the time a guy gets interested in adult dramas where at least *some* of the men show they have balls, he is an adult who hopefully has grown some balls of his own. In the meantime, you young guys want to watch wild action movies where the heroic men are really just Bad Boys but fighting for the "right side." They break all the rules and take crazy chances with their lives— but for all the right reasons. Think of the cop movies where the renegade hero is the only one who really knows what is going on. His boss is an idiot (again, no mature leader). So, without any mature guidance, he goes out on his own but comes out on top. There's a theme: False balls with good results. Would it be that boring to have movies portraying mature leaders teaching younger men how to operate in the world?

But its not just young guys who get caught up in the chase for what turn out to be false balls. We regular guys, in the real world, are not superheroes, but we can do some pretty outrageous things to fight off the doofus image that Cartoon Man and Sit-Com Moron have given us for a role model. We can show off. We can act like Bad Boys. We can be smart-asses with attitude. We can do all sorts of stupid things—anything to separate us from the crowd of boring Nice Guys who obey all the rules and get walked on by (non-Worthwhile) women. We can take foolish chances, risking our lives and other people's lives—sometimes losing them—in a weak imitation of a superhero. The guys too scared to rebel out in the open can be sneaky. They can cheat and steal, then lie to get away with it. But every time they succeed, their ball-less self-esteem takes a hit.

As boys, we need outlets for our power and passion. We are ripe, physically and emotionally, for drama. Unfortunately, this makes us suckers for other people's causes. Girls wanting babies offer us the opportunity to *become men* by impregnating them. I certainly understand the urge to take them up on the offer of sex, but boys who believe that spreading your seed around the neighborhood is proof of manhood leave the rest of us to deal with a crop of sad and angry fatherless babies.

Politicians needing soldiers to fight their wars (be they right or wrong) know exactly whom to approach: Boys needing to make the transition into manhood. These guys—guys like *you*—are ripe for being sent into battle. They're ready to be given a cause to fight for so they can earn their balls. I mean no disrespect to soldiers here. I appreciate the military when appropriately deployed for a righteous reason—like to defend their country. However, take note that politicians don't always start wars for righteous reasons. They also don't go after mature men to become new soldiers. Mature men think too much and have too much life experience to be molded into soldiers who won't question orders. A mature man thinks before he puts his precious life on the line. That is, after all, the ultimate conscious compromise. So, younger, less experienced men are targeted, especially guys raised in poverty, for whom "three hots and a cot" seems like a good deal.

Traditionally, the military has played a useful role in society, specializing in turning boys into men. In the right circumstances, it can do a good job. It has all the requisite elements: The situation being trained for (battle) is stressful and requires taking risks, the cause is for something greater than oneself (peers, the country, a system of thought), and the opportunities for challenging the self—managing and perhaps conquering fear—are many. However, military services don't need everyone to do a stint—which is good because the service isn't right for everybody. Just like society only needs so many cops and firemen, we only need so many soldiers. So, we need to take the "balls issue" out of the high-drama arenas. Again, here's the gold standard to remember:

A man grows balls by doing the right thing *because it is the right thing to do*.

It's as simple as that—and as hard—because that is a damn high standard. Boys and young men can't hold to that standard consistently enough to hold on to their balls. This is why boys and young men aren't ready to be husbands and fathers.

Every kid deserves to have a mature man—with balls—as a father. It doesn't mean Dad isn't going to make mistakes and have some weak moments. Maturity doesn't mean perfection. Mature men make bad decisions and fall into old, immature behaviors now and then. That's normal too. But mature men either catch themselves as they fall off track or handle like men the consequences of their actions. Admitting your mistakes and making them right is part of doing the right thing because it is the right thing to do.

That's how you grow and keep your balls.

CHAPTER FOUR

Why Women Love Jerks

Actually, it's not quite that simple. To say that "women love jerks" is a whiny excuse "Nice Guys" use to explain why they're not getting laid. "Gee, *I* could be a jerk too and get all the women I want, but I'm not that kind of guy."

Stop. Don't say that; don't even think it. You're just embarrassing yourself.

True, it appears that women don't get turned on by Nice Guys. True, it seems the guys who act like jerks get lots of female attention. Nice Guys have been noticing this for generations. Women, to greater or lesser degrees, *are* attracted to the "Bad Boy" style. So what? Guys are attracted to sluts. We're even.

Trust me on this one—you can take it to the bank: *Women don't want real Bad Boys for husbands any more than men want real sluts for wives.* What men *and* women want from their partners is some excitement, some passion, and some confidence. Nice alone is boring but nice with passion, now *that's* the trick and the ticket for a successful, long-term relationship. But few men are raised with an emphasis on developing their passions.

As men, we're culturally programmed to be good providers first and foremost. We are expected to follow the rules at school and at work, get good grades, find good jobs, get promoted if we can, and stay out of trouble. To carve out our slice of the American Dream, we sacrifice our personal dreams (where our passion lies) to be good providers. Does that sound fun? It's not. It's honorable, sure, but not very interesting.

Worthwhile Women, as they are maturing, may chase after Bad Boys (or wish they had) but will finally settle for the nice guy—we make loyal husbands and great fathers, after-all—but if we don't excite their passions, they'll forever pine away for the passion of the Bad Boy. Nice Guys know this, and it makes us crazy. We watch women getting cheated on or otherwise abused by their Bad Boy boyfriends or husbands and just shake our heads. We can't make any sense of it. But instead of becoming powerful and passionate ourselves, we get jealous—and mad at our partners for being attracted to the passion in other men.

So Nice Guys are in a pickle. What do we do with our wild side while we're busy being so good and doing what is expected of us? What do we do with the churning energy we had as boys (that sometimes got us into trouble)? You can only stuff that energy down for so long.

What do we do? We "act out." We rebel in stupid ways against all these rules and expectations. We do something we're not supposed to do. We have some secrets we share only with our friends, if anyone. We hope not to get caught.

The healthiest among us find a good outlet for our wild sides. We get into hobbies or sports with our buddies and feel good about our ever-growing talents and skills. Some of the rest of us fall back on drinking or using drugs, keeping our wild energy in check by getting loaded. I'm talking about more than just cutting loose now and then with your friends. If we overdo alcohol, for example, we may get the opposite of what we want. Rather than taming our wild side so that we mellow out and act like we "don't care anymore," the alcohol fuels our fire. Our wild (and angry) energy catches fire and wreaks havoc on our lives. You've seen the t-shirt that says, "Instant Asshole: Just add Alcohol," right? It's only funny because we all know guys just like that. Other guys have an opposite reaction, but a sad one. They get loaded and more or less disappear from their families, hiding out in their garages.

You have some wild energy in you; we all do. What do you do with it? Some of us get stubborn about silly things: like cleaning up after ourselves or otherwise not doing our share of chores at home. The gross guys have bad hygiene. These are the guys who haven't yet figured out that women aren't into guys that smell like dirty laundry and old farts. Actually, these greasy-haired guys aren't ready for girlfriends anyway, so maybe the smelly, rumpled look works for them.

Those of us who have gotten into committed relationships before we've figured out how to handle our wild energy sometimes do irresponsible things we later regret. We gamble money we can't afford to lose. We cheat on our partners (and usually get caught), we drink and drive—that sort of thing. None of this is very smart but it's our mistake to make. There's freedom in being irresponsible; at least, for a while. In fact, Nice Guys are kind of like the girls who take control of their otherwise over-managed lives by starving themselves. They don't have the power or skills to take charge of their relationships, but they can decide when and how much to eat—or not.

The problem with this kind of acting out is that it does nothing to raise a guy's self-esteem. How is he supposed to develop his personal power and passion while stubbornly insisting on drinking beer and watching sports all weekend while his wife or girlfriend wonders when they're ever going to do anything fun together? He's gone from being a Nice Guy to a beer-bellied slug.

Meanwhile, what does the Bad Boy have to offer a woman? For one thing, he is interesting. He clearly isn't following the rules. Everyone is taught to follow the rules. Despite all the warnings of negative consequences, he does what he wants to do. That's pretty exciting, even if he makes bad choices and gets into trouble. Where, women wonder, does he get the idea that he can act like this and get away with it? How can he not care what the world thinks about him? He seems amazing, free of society's rules—and that is attractive. His very style shows passion.

Check out the differences in behavior between Nice Guys and Bad Boys: When it comes to women, the Bad Boy acts like he doesn't need them at all while the Nice Guys (without balls) are tripping over their own feet trying to get the courage together just to say hello. Who looks like he has more personal power? Who looks more interesting to be around?

Nice Guys worship women. This is *wrong*. Women don't deserve to be worshipped—*and they know it*. Their shit stinks; they're just human, plain and simple, and frankly don't feel understood by a guy who treats them like royalty. They think he's a chump. The few women who do believe they are princesses and expect to be treated that way are to be avoided like the plague.

No woman respects a man who worships her. I'm not talking about appreciating a good woman and treating her well. I'm not talking about love either. You're supposed to love your woman. Loving is not worshipping. Worshipping is what is meant by the expression of "putting a woman on a pedestal." Worthwhile Women hate that and avoid the men who do it.

Worthwhile Women feel sorry for guys like this. Other less mature women will smile to your face, let you buy drinks and dinner and presents, all the while looking over your shoulder for some guy who will turn them on.

Nice Guys would do well to treat women like people. People deserve to be treated with respect. That's good enough. That's what Nice Guys with balls do. They don't pretend to be assholes to get women. Their self-confidence and passion for life bring them plenty of female attention.

Bad Boys have other advantages over passionless Nice Guys. Bad Boys have an air of mystery to them. This intrigues women. They are immediately fascinated by the Bad Boy's life story. They want to gain his trust and be the "special one" he opens up to. They want to save him from himself. This is very exciting. Bad Boys are exciting.

Passionless Nice Guys, in comparison, put women to sleep. They may like the Nice Guy, but they're not going to fantasize about him when he's not around. Besides which, women have their secret sides too. Whether or not she acts it out, the average woman also gets in the mood, now and then, to break a few rules, to be irresponsible, and generally go against what is expected of her. When she gets in that mood, who's going to be more fun to be with? The guy who worships the ground she walks on? I don't think so. Without a passionate and fun (and nice) guy to go a little nuts with, a woman will opt for the Bad Boy. Can you blame her?

Women have sexual fantasies too, and despite the common wisdom on the subject, not all of those fantasies are beach scenes at dusk with a mysterious handsome man riding up on a white horse. Even nice girls can be plenty freaky. The woman has to ask herself: If I show my wild side, will it be too much for this Nice Guy to handle? Will he judge me for having a wild side? Will I have to hide it from him? Will he even notice if I send him the "Go!" sign? Or will he ruin the mood by asking for my permission each step of the way?

At least the Bad Boy is up front with his craziness, and he's good at spotting a woman's signals. Women know that they don't have to wonder what he is up to—most of the time he's up to no good—but at least he's fun and interesting. As long as he respects "No" when it is seriously said, he's a good bet for good time.

I know what you're thinking and you're wrong. The answer is *not* to become a Bad Boy. I know there are people who disagree and will tell you that becoming a Bad Boy (or learning to act like one) is *exactly* what you should do. Truthfully, taking that route, in the short run, will probably get you laid—lots of women hungry for a break from ball-less Nice Guys will respond to it—but that plan comes with a great deal of baggage and risk. For one thing, be prepared to lie to women and to mess with their heads in ways that can seriously backfire on you. We'll talk about those situations later. Plus, you can't really *decide to become* a Bad Boy. That happens for a reason. Real Bad Boys aren't acting. They didn't have happy or safe childhoods. Their "I don't give a damn about other people" attitude grew out of somewhere, usually because people who should have given more of a damn about them when they were kids didn't. This is the heart of the Bad Boy's mystery. It is his private pain; the pain he shows by making other people's lives miserable. It is what a girl hopes he will share with only her, making her the only one who really understands him.

Now, we *all* grew up with some pain in our lives. But however attractive the Bad Boy lifestyle may seem, if you are a Nice Guy by nature, you were, as a child, taken care of better than he was. Ironically, the Bad Boy deserves the understanding and nurturing that women want to give him, but he's usually too wounded to take it in. He doesn't trust it. By *acting* like a Bad Boy, you won't fool anybody. You'll just look like an asshole. So forget it.

The answer, fortunately, is much simpler, infinitely more honest and will still get you laid: *Get some passion in your life.* Do things that make you feel proud of yourself. Try new things. Take on challenges. Stop envying other people who are richer or better looking than you are. Stop feeling sorry for yourself. Stop making excuses for why you are not happier. Instead, put together a plan that aims you in a direction that interests and excites you. Whatever it takes, keep some passion in your blood. Following your passion, even in little steps, will raise your spirits and make you proud of yourself. Stick to your values. Act with integrity. People will notice, and your reputation as an honest man will grow. So will your confidence—and that, along with your passion, will make you attractive to Worthwhile Women. You will be able to see women for what they are: people. And you won't be risking your self-worth when you approach one.

You don't have to turn your life upside down in one day. You don't have to quit your day job. The trick is having balance in your life. Be responsible when you need to be, but let yourself cut loose now and then and be a little crazy. You'll be happier. Besides, Worthwhile Women want balance in their men. They want a responsible guy who treats them well but who also has a wild side. They don't want to be able to predict his every move. That's boring. A man with some passion is open to what the world has to offer. He'll try new things because doing so is interesting for *him.* He can't try to be different for her. She'll know he isn't being sincere.

Women in general, let alone Worthwhile Women, don't want men who will put up with their bitchiness without complaint. (Even Worthwhile Women get bitchy). A *chronically* bitchy woman is begging her man to set some limits. But she can't tell him that. He has to figure it out for himself or he's both hopeless and useless to her, other than as a human wallet. She may rebel against his first attempts at limit setting (especially at the beginning) and threaten to leave—which is fine if you consider the alternative.

What man with *any* balls will voluntarily live with a chronically bitchy woman? You have to set your limits, state clearly what you will tolerate and what you won't, and she must respond adequately or the relationship has to end. If she responds well (meaning, she stops acting so bitchy so often), then life goes on, and happily so. If she doesn't, you're better off without her. Set your limits and draw lines and stick to them—there's nothing more pathetic than a guy who sets limits and then backs off of them. But *never* allow yourself to get violent with a partner. I don't care how shitty she behaves. She's responsible for her behavior and you're responsible for yours. Don't hit a woman; if things have gotten that bad, break up with her.

There are women who *expect* their men to get violent with them. Usually, this kind of woman saw violence in her parent's relationship. She has been in violent relationships before. To her, violence in a relationship is normal. She may push and provoke your rage until you feel violent urges rising within you. **This is definitely the time to leave and find a different woman.** No woman is worth giving up your values for. No woman is worth your self-respect *or your freedom*. It doesn't matter why she acts this way. Let her go to therapy and work it out. In truth, she probably won't. Instead, she'll just find another man whose self-control isn't as good as yours and find herself "victimized" again. That's a whole weird drama you want to avoid at all costs.

As a powerful and passionate man, you will want the same in your woman too. The allure of the girl-next-door type is the secret, wild part of her you hope is there. It's great and desirable for a woman to be good in the typical ways, like being smart, capable, and responsible. But we want a woman to have access to her Bad Girl qualities too. We want our women to have a secret (at least *slightly* slutty) side only *we* get to experience. We want Worthwhile Women, and they come complete with passion *and* a wild side—a little nasty edge. That edge comes out as bitchiness now and then, and assuming we men aren't the cause of that bitchiness—and sometimes we are—they rely on us to show some balls and manage it for them. It makes women feel safe when we set limits. They love it.

So, enough complaining about women only liking jerks. Truthfully, the jerks, the Bad Boys, have a lot to teach their ball-less Nice Guy brothers. Bad Boys don't worship women. They have their opinions and they express them without apology. They don't live in fear of making mistakes or being wrong. Those concerns are low on their list.

Men with personal power—with balls—are in the middle of the spectrum, while Nice Guys and Bad Boys hold down—and are stuck in—the two opposite extremes. This is the great truth my friends and I now understand. And we're in our forties. Don't wait as long as we did to get clear on this. When we fantasize, "If I only knew then what I know now," we mean knowing about the joys of the center. We didn't know that by developing skills, knowledge, and courage—Growing Balls—we would gain confidence, self-esteem, *and* the attention of girls.

CHAPTER FIVE

What to Do With Your Dick

The short version:

- If your religion tries to put you at war with your dick, don't let it.
- Masturbation is normal; don't believe anyone who tells you otherwise.
- Western culture is totally screwed up about sex.
- Learn to flirt. It's a dying art.
- Just because you can get laid doesn't mean you should.
- Always wear a condom.
- Don't have sex with crazy girls and *never* with an underage girl.
- Talk about sex with someone you trust.
- You alone are responsible for what you do with your dick.

The Long Version:

The fantasy advice of "What to Do with Your Dick" is not practical. Our dicks, if left in charge, would have us nail everything in sight—which, admittedly, sounds fun. That temptation to give sexual responsibility over to our little heads has proved overwhelming to many boys and men, with widely varying degrees of success.

It turns out that just because you *can* get laid doesn't mean you necessarily *should*. We guys tend to grow up thinking that being a man means cashing in on all sexual opportunities. Many women expect this of us too and are *shocked* if we turn down sex. A mature man knows this is ridiculous—sometimes you have to take a pass—while young horny guys, especially virgins, can hardly *imagine* saying no to *any* offer of sex. However, no matter what your friends may say, there are definitely times when you should turn down sex . . . but we'll get into that later.

Recreational sex, as fun as it can be, is a risky game, especially if you don't know your partner well (or at all). Keep this in mind: if your hot little honey gets pregnant, what happens next *will not be up to you*. Whether she has the baby (keeping it or giving it away for adoption) or gets an abortion is strictly *her* decision. Fair or not, legally speaking, you are going to be the bystander holding on white-knuckled to your wallet, waiting to find out if you are in for eighteen long expensive years of child support and legal responsibility.

That's just the start of it; there's much more. We haven't even begun to look at the other complications a dick-based decision may give you. Consider your feelings, for one thing; especially about actually becoming somebody's dad—a parent—until the day you die. Remember, all kids deserve and need the protection and love and mature guidance of a real father. If you get scared and decide to duck out on *that* responsibility, it may very well haunt you for the rest of your life. Plus, you will have put another sad, angry, and fatherless kid (with low self-esteem) into society, leaving the rest of us to deal with your problem. Give us a break, okay? Society has enough troubles already. And one more thing: this girl who gave you a fun roll without even using birth control: *Is she your choice to be the mother to your child?*

Okay, so that's the pregnancy part. Birth control can (usually) handle that issue, right? Well, sure, as long as both of you are honest and consistent about it. You better know her well enough to trust her about something so important. Keep in mind: Birth control methods can fail. Even the Pill can fail. So if your girl is being honest and consistent in taking it, there are other medicines she may be taking which will render the Pill ineffective. You better hope she is reading all the labels and is on top of these things. Better yet, always use a condom. Always.

If it helps any, keep in mind that any ex-virgin will admit that despite his adolescent thinking that his world would never be the same after finally "getting some," the sun actually rose normally the next day. Sure, he was happy to be a member of the Club, but in truth, he was still the same guy after losing his virginity.

Want to know what changes your life permanently? Finding out you're going to be a father—that will do it. So will being told you now have an incurable venereal disease or you've infected someone you care about. Now you're both damaged goods—forever. You really have to think these things through *ahead of time*—before the blood drains from your big head into the little one.

"What to Do With Your Dick" is not a chapter meant to talk you out of recreational sex altogether, despite how it may read. Fortunately, there is a middle ground between brainless sport-fucking and chastity. You don't have to wind up a twenty-something virgin with calluses on your palms. To help you navigate that gray area, here are a few questions to think through to decide what to do with your dick.

1. What's the hurry?

If you have to make up your mind fast—right now—in order to get laid, skip it. If getting laid means taking unnecessary risks *right now* or losing your chance altogether, the answer is easy: Lose it. Be happy and proud that you had the chance in the first place. You're obviously doing something right. Feel good about knowing *you could have gotten laid*. You will have other chances. Better to go home and masturbate (again, I know) than to be stuck with the consequences of a little-head decision. One warning if you follow this advice: Expect to second-guess yourself. Expect to kick yourself later for turning down the sex. Expect to regret the day you started reading "that stupid book."

Know that your dick will call you stupid, because the odds for a great time and even a happy ending are usually in your favor. Your friends may say the same thing. Guys you trust, maybe even your own father, may think you should have gone for it. Doesn't matter. Don't be rushed, bullied, forced, or coerced into sex. Ever. No one but you lives with the consequences of what you do with your dick.

2. What is your stand on abortion? What is hers?

Let's say your partner-to-be says she would have an abortion if she got pregnant. Do you know her well enough to believe her? Do you leave birth control up to her or do you take care of it yourself? (This is another no-brainer, right? You're going to wear a condom.) Your girl may believe what she tells you, but a month or so later when she pees on that little test stick and it says she's going to be a *mommy*, well; even *she* can't predict how she is going to feel. And she'll likely have plenty of support for changing her mind and keeping the baby. You can't say, "Hey, wait a second, you promised . . ." Don't bother. You'll just sound stupid. Meanwhile, even if she *is* telling the truth about birth control—let's say she is on the Pill—you move on to the next unromantic but vital question about what to do with your dick.

3. Do you *ever* fuck without a condom?

Just because I told you to always use one doesn't mean you're going to listen to me or actually follow through. So let's talk this through a little, okay? I want you to *own* your decision. So, if we're not talking about unwanted pregnancies, we must be talking about the nasty health concerns of riding bareback.

First of all, I know that you hear about sexually transmitted diseases all the time. You must get tired of being warned that sex can kill you. As a man in my forties, I find it sad that you have to worry so much about health problems and sex. My generation only had to worry about accidental pregnancy and *curable* venereal diseases. We sweated the embarrassment of having to go to the doctor's office or clinic for *the cure*—which seems almost quaint now—or like a joke. When genital herpes came around, we *really* freaked out because it was our first incurable venereal disease. But even herpes was quickly made more or less controllable and it certainly was not fatal or even life threatening.

But times have changed—and I'm not just talking about AIDS here either. Hepatitis C will wreck your liver, and if you don't get a new one, eventually kill you. But death aside (if you *can* put it aside), there are other incurable, gnarly diseases out there waiting for you to catch and spread around. Consider this horrid little scenario: You find yourself in an unexpected sexual situation with a willing girl. You want to be a player, so you decide to scam on your steady girlfriend, even though you don't have a condom available. The scamming issue is between you and her (you probably aren't ready for a steady girlfriend, anyway); but do you want to be responsible for accidentally giving your girlfriend, let's say, Chlamydia? That's an STD undetectable to you (and the girl) but one that, untreated, will eventually leave both your quick score and your girlfriend sterile—no kids of their own, ever. Or, how about a dose of venereal warts? Those are also hard to detect (they're not big like the ones you get on your hands) so they get spread quickly and easily. They also greatly increase a woman's chances of getting cervical cancer—a proven killer of young women. They also can affect her future children during childbirth. Are you thinking about these things when easy sex knocks on your door?

I didn't think so.

Fun is fun, sure, but you want to be able to look yourself in the mirror, don't you? So: When a chance to get laid unexpectedly shows up—and you don't have a condom—what do you do? There are lots of clean girls out there, right? The odds say she's probably one of them. Do you take your chances and go for it? Do you get loaded, get busy, and play the odds? I'm really asking here—do you?

If you say, "Well, it depends . . ." I now must beat my head bloody against the wall. Really? It *depends*? Depends on what? How hot she is? What your friends will say (or think) about you if you pass it up? Dude, please, you have to think this through. It is just this kind of situation that tests your values. This is why you need to have them in order before you leave the house. You can't stick to values when you don't even know what they are. The pressure to buckle in can be tremendous.

Maybe you're worried about what *she'll* think or say. Some girls feel rejected or insulted if you turn them down. Believing that *any* guy will go for *any* sex that comes his way, this girl might take it personally when you take a pass. Things could get ugly. She might even lie about what happened or about you. Hell, she might tell her friends she thinks you're gay. But hey, if she's that wacky, be glad you took a pass. Trust me, at some point she would have made your life miserable. This is not a girl you want to be the mother of your children. She is not on her way to becoming a Worthwhile Woman. Meanwhile, we're talking about a potentially life-changing decision here.

This sexual situation should be a no-brainer, right? Logically, yes. But in the real world, this is a tough situation for any guy, especially if alcohol or other drugs are involved. No one thinks straight when they're loaded. For a virgin who has been waiting for his chance to get laid, this fork in the road is a brutal decision. But trust me, you'd be an idiot to tune out all you know and just hope for the best. Sex is great and all, but be serious. Imagine if it turned out bad. You'd wish you could turn back the clock but you never can. You don't want to lie sleepless in bed asking yourself endless questions that start with, "I wish," "Why didn't I . . . ?", and "If only I had . . ."

You can't be confused by sweet clean-looking girls either. Sometimes, the easy, unexpected sex comes from a girl who's looking to get over being dumped by some other guy. Nothing raises her self-esteem like grabbing the attention of another guy—like you. But who knows what her last boyfriend was up to and with whom? In general, just because the girl you meet seems to be a "nice girl" doesn't mean she was sexually responsible before hooking up with you.

Remember that some of the nastiest diseases don't have obvious outward symptoms for the woman. She may think she is healthy when she is not. The pill won't keep you safe from what she has. Only a condom (fresh and used properly) will protect you. Keep this in mind too: she doesn't know what kind of nasty viruses *you* may be about to give *her*. If she doesn't know you very well (or at all) but is willing to ride barebacked with you anyway, what does that tell you about *her*? No matter how cool she seems to be, think about how many guys have already been where you are about to go. Do you think she screened them any better than she is screening you? Do you trust those guys to have been careful with their dicks? You don't think she is making a special exception just for you, do you? Trust me, stud: You're not that irresistible. She's either stupid, not thinking straight (did we mention alcohol?), or depressed. Maybe she's been around the track a few too many times and doesn't really care about what happens to her anymore. Or maybe she really *wants a baby*—someone for her to love and to love her back—and she needs your sperm. And you're just thinking about having a few beers and getting laid!

Here's my advice: If she doesn't seem to care about herself, don't do it. Run. She's trouble. Don't do it, especially if she claims to *love you*. She doesn't know what love is any more than you do and you're headed for no end to problems with this girl.

Still not convinced? Can't let this one get away? Got one hand on your zipper? Okay. But if you've thought about this ahead of time, you can *still* use the big head before surrendering to the little one. You don't have to do *everything* with her; in the heat of the moment, you can stick to oral sex (still potentially risky, but under the circumstances, a much better and safer choice) or good old hands-on safe sex. That will relieve the pressure in the immediate circumstances and give you a chance to think more clearly—and no one gets into any trouble. That isn't too complicated, is it?

Okay, moving on. Let's say you have the pregnancy and health issue covered.

4. When it comes to sex, how old is old enough for you or for her?

The quick answer is the legal one, meaning the "age of consent." Each state has rules about how old you have to be to supposedly understand what you are doing when it comes to sex so that you can "consent" to it. The longer answer has to do with what we have already covered—the readiness to take the risks involved with being sexually active.

So, if you're both legal adults, no problems here. If not, however, you have *big* problems and so does society. We have a huge problem in this country with adult men having sex with under-aged girls. These guys rarely take care of their offspring and the rest of us get stuck with that job and expense.

But even if you don't care about society, you really don't want to be on the wrong side of the law when it comes to sex. Even if a minor consents to having sex with you, *even if she wants it,* that sex is called statutory *rape.* Don't even bother arguing the point. It's a black-and-white legal issue.

Ethics aside, sex with a minor is a numbers game in every state (age and difference in age of the participants) and the rules of that game are very clear. You're guilty or you aren't. If you two get caught, or if she starts to feel guilty (or angry) and tells someone what you two did, you're toast. Or if she gets in trouble and needs to sacrifice you to take the pressure off her, she can do just that. She can even make something up and accuse you of forcing her to have sex—she can change history—and, buddy, you're screwed. Who do you think people are going to believe, her with those big sad eyes, or you, standing there with your dick in your hands? You do the math. Even if she tries to protect you, her parents can decide to press charges. There's nothing you can do about it. Where you'll be living, it ain't safe bending over to pick up the soap.

That's the legal side of the issue. The other question to ask yourself, if you are an adult having sex with underage girls is, "What the hell is wrong with me?"

An adult hooking up with underage girls has, as we say in the therapy biz, "issues." It is one thing to notice and appreciate sexy teenagers. That's normal. There's no law against being attracted to them, but there are plenty of laws against acting on that attraction.

Let's limit this discussion to attraction for teenagers, not children. It is normal and okay to be turned on by the newest sexy teen-queen on MTV. **However, it is absolutely *not normal* to be turned on by children.** If kids turn you on sexually, you really do have psychological issues. Get yourself to a therapist *now* before you hurt somebody. I'm serious about this. Help and relief are available. Don't wait until you mess up other peoples' lives and get yourself into serious trouble.

Adult men who actually approach underage girls (teenagers, not kids) need to grow up and grow some balls. Going after underage girls is a sign of a man's emotional weakness. An adult, mature woman wants an adult, mature man. The guy who chases underage girls doesn't have the confidence to approach women his own age (or at least, "of legal age"). If you are one of these guys, you need to get smart fast. It's okay to be immature but it's not okay to act on it. In other words, work on growing up and leave the underage girls alone. The only young girls who will want you are trouble anyway. They are the ones most likely to lie about birth control (because they usually *want* babies). They have more emotional problems, as a group. They're going to be clingy and needy and drive you nuts in no time.

Most teenage/underage girls have the sense to stick to boys their own age. They know that men who pursue them are "creepy." Still, there are teenage girls who confuse their ability to attract older guys with evidence of their own maturity. These girls take themselves way too seriously. They get their feelings hurt easily. It is tough on their egos to realize how wrong they are about themselves and the older guys they choose. By the time they figure it out, they're lucky to escape from the experience without a pregnancy or STD because the guy who goes after younger girls is usually irresponsible with his dick.

If you have been going after underage girls, it's time to grow up. You have low self-esteem (sorry for the therapist lingo, but its true). *You* are the needy one, not her. You need to focus on building your self-esteem on your own and *by yourself* instead of relying on adoring young girls to feed your ego. Get really good at something; it will help you to feel proud of yourself. Challenge yourself with difficult projects. Set some goals and achieve them.

This is not easy and will require a good deal of focus and self-discipline, but the pay-off is excellent and just what you need. Do what I'm telling you and you will find yourself *attracting women your own age*—without really trying. They will be turned on to *you*—because **women are turned on to powerful men**. Mature, Worthwhile Women don't like needy men. Needy men are pathetic and ball-less, and women know it.

5. Are you emotionally ready for sex? Is she?

You won't consider this a problem at all if you're sure you are ready. And that's fine. Maybe you are ready, and maybe not. *Don't confuse desire with readiness.* If you have nagging doubts, be honest with yourself and pay attention to them. You might try talking to someone you trust that may know you better than you know yourself.

For argument's sake, however, let's assume you *are* ready to get laid. Great. Now think of the girl. The "hottie" you successfully pick up and casually *boink* is more than a warm playground for your dick. She is a real person with an emotional history and a complex set of feelings. Just because she looks good (okay, great) doesn't mean she's ready for sex with you (even if she's had sex before); nor does it mean she's healthy upstairs. Ask any sexually experienced guy if he ever ended up in bed with a hot-looking nut job, and then sit back and settle in for a horrible story.

Just because you walk away from the sex with a clean dick (and she didn't get pregnant), you still might have problems. What if you decide that she's not right for you (even to date) but she falls for you big time? Consider this scenario: She told you she just wanted to have some fun. You believed her. After all, other girls have told you this and it worked out fine. But this girl is different. She's fooling herself but *you* don't know that. *You don't have a clue* what's going on in that pretty head of hers. Truthfully, she may not either. Before you had sex, she probably said a few weird things that got your attention at the time. These were red flags, but you ignored them, which is always a mistake. Why did you ignore them? Easy answer: She was giving you the green light for sex and so was your dick. You were thinking with the little head.

"Well, so what if she falls for me?" you say. "That's *her* problem, isn't it? I'll tell her I'm not into her anymore and we'll both move on, right?"

If only. Wait until she starts hassling you. Your phone starts ringing off the hook. Listen in horror as she twists your words—what you said to get laid—and turns them into broken promises. She'll be crying and begging for more of your attention; and when you tell her again that you're through, she turns on you like a viper, bitching at you and making very ugly threats. Now she is turning your life into a nightmare. Like the girl in the movie *Swim Fan*, or from my generation, the horrifying woman in the movie *Fatal Attraction,* your hottie has turned into the psycho bitch from hell. Shit like this happens every day.

If it happens to you, remember: I tried to warn you. Talk to your more sexually experienced buddies. Every guy knows some poor bastard who has gone through this, if he hasn't himself. One experience even *a little* like this example will convince you to use the bigger head for thinking next time

The long and short of it is this: *Emotions do count*—both hers and yours. You have to factor them in to your decision making when it comes to what to do with your dick. Thoughtless sex, however, is just stupid. It's way too risky for the short-term benefit. Under the right circumstances, sex is *so good* that you don't want to blow it by choosing the wrong time or the wrong person and end up with regrets, especially for your first time.

Note to virgins: You only lose your virginity once. How well or how poorly it goes can color your sexual confidence for a long time. So, set yourself up for sexual success and remember: Just because you *can* get laid doesn't mean you *should*.

* * *

As you've no doubt already surmised, there is no shortage of people who will tell you what to do with your dick (although they may use different terms, eh?). Your family, religion, or culture (or a combination of the three) has standards of sexual behavior and you *know* you are expected to follow them. If you're lucky—and most men are *not*—these expectations fit with the urges and desires of your body and mind. Instead, most of us have to decide which of these expectations and rules we're going to follow and which we're going to ignore, or lie about. This means finding a balance between *schtupping* everyone in sight and being celibate. While there's a lot of territory in between these extremes, it's not easy finding open-minded people to talk to about sex.

Masturbation: Your Friend

I can't think of any good that has come from going to war with your body. You have to breathe, eat, drink, and sleep. Those are no-brainers, first-order "can't ignore" imperatives. To give up on one of those is to guarantee death. The only question is how long, from minutes to weeks.

The one biological urge that isn't on that "must do" list but is number one on the next "nearly as important" list is sex. Many people will counsel you about sex with one simple piece of advice: Stay a virgin until you get married. If that's what you want and you can pull it off (pardon the pun), well, case closed. You're in luck because life as a bachelor will be fairly simple for you, assuming you can successfully tackle the masturbation question. For our purposes here, if you're in that group, you can now stop reading this chapter and move on to the next one.

For everyone else, there's more to consider.

For guys, once we hit puberty, we *have* to have regular sexual release. We can do it alone (and pretty much all of us do), we can have sex *with* someone (or some*thing*, if you're kinky), or we can keep ignoring our sexual urges—in which case our bodies eventually take over as we sleep and we wake up from hot dreams on a cold spot. That pretty much sums up our choices.

Ask any guy if he thinks sex is important. Unless he has forgotten the location of his balls altogether, he'll tell you that it is. Unfortunately, once we have had it and we're no longer getting enough (or any) sex, it tends to become *too* important. We get frustrated, our self-esteem suffers, and we end up acting crazy in some other area of our lives. We become jerks at work or at home. Or we get depressed. We get too loaded too often on whatever substance we like. Or we get fat. Maybe we'll cheat. Women know this about us. Since all guys are different, how much sex is enough depends on whom you ask, but you can count on this: an unhappy dick is attached to an unhappy guy.

*　　*　　*

Why Is Sex Everywhere You Look?

You can argue that if we're still in the grip of the Puritans who founded this country (my apologies to the Native Americans who were here first), sex should be more of a private subject. But it's not; it's very public. In fact, it is everywhere you look. Sex absolutely rules advertising. It is paraded on the cover of countless magazines, and I don't just mean the soft—and hard-core skin magazines. Sex is the theme of a majority of television shows and movies. And it has always been this way—it's just far less subtle nowadays.

Why is sex such a big deal and not a more private matter? Our culture loudly rebels against our Puritan roots. What is going on? The answer isn't rocket science: In our childhood, we pick up a good dose of Puritanism. We get in trouble if we even talk about sex at school. Even before we, as kids, know what sex is, we know it is not for us. Our parents are usually too embarrassed to talk about it. The cultural message is: "Sex is taboo, forbidden; it is wrong and dirty." At the same time, kids see sex paraded everywhere in the cultural landscape and see the interest people have in it. We're not even supposed to ask about sex when we're young. The conversation starts only after we're old enough to have been thoroughly misinformed about it by our peers.

But kids are just young, curious people. As such, they are attracted to things forbidden. Rigid rules just make them more curious and hungry for the forbidden fruit. No wonder we grow up to be turned on by sex outside the rules. So we break them outright, especially when we see others doing it without bolts of lightning striking them down. Basically, sex is a big, public deal in our culture because it is not embraced as the natural, healthy, and powerful driving force it truly is in our lives.

As a culture, we're no different from the kid who is warned not to masturbate or he'll go blind or go to hell or just be considered an immoral person. We rebel from these dire warnings, but in stupid ways. For example, our goofy Puritan roots show when gaudy violence—all the blood, gore, and guts you want—is allowed on public airwaves so long as there are no nipples, never mind penises or vaginas, on the television screen. It's crazy. I'm not arguing for airing skin flicks on primetime network television, but how screwed up are we to think that given the choice of our boys watching sex or violence on television, violence is the *less harmful* of the two?

Religions have always struggled with sex, which testifies to its power. Fundamentalist Islamic culture so distrusts a man's libido that it cloaks its women behind a wall of dark cloth so they will be less of a temptation to the men who, incidentally, *are* raised to be at war with their dicks. Again, the more you make sex a forbidden fruit, the more powerful it becomes and the hungrier people become for it. By covering women from head to toe, they become objects of obsession.

The best evidence of this is the promise to the young terrorist suicide bombers of *seventy-two virgins* in heaven as a reward for martyrdom. (Personally, I would prefer experienced women who know what they are doing in bed, but that's just me). Now, glancing over an outdoor magazine stand stocked full of photos of luscious, young female flesh, I can and will admit understanding how immoral we Westerners look to the religious fundamentalist. We *do* appear sex-obsessed as a culture, and arguably, spiritually lost. Fair enough. But fundamentalist Islamic claims of moral purity for burka-draped women lose credibility in light of them being promised as heavenly sex toys to martyrs.

But we have some of this crazy and hypocritical thinking here at home too. U. S. criminal courts used to allow attorneys to blame women in court for getting raped because they were wearing sexy outfits at the time of the assault. This was a legal travesty that has only recently changed. Nonetheless, many people still think a woman who dresses in a sexy outfit has it coming to her. Those are *our culture's* fundamentalist roots showing. Certainly, modesty has its place, as does common sense. Girls need to know there *are* men out there who will assume things about them based upon how they are dressed. But this doesn't excuse sexual assault. Which brings us to the final point:

Under all circumstances, a man is responsible for what he does with his dick.

Despite all the problems caused by the way our Western culture deals with sex, the system remains more or less unchanged. Kids still learn about sex on playgrounds, in bad dirty jokes that have most of the facts wrong. Kids get in trouble at home and at school for using sexual words, making sexual jokes or showing sexual curiosity.

Parents don't have to be religious fundamentalists to unwittingly teach their kids that sex is wrong and dirty. By warning them about how *other people* may interpret their sexually oriented words and behaviors, they fill the subject of sex with curiosity and make it powerful. And through this, the Puritan grip on our culture survives.

There is a harmlessly kinky side to all of this. I admit there is *some fun* in being purposefully *naughty* when it comes to sex, but this sly and playful benefit is too small for all the trouble that comes with it. Putting boys at war with their dicks is emotional terrorism and can lead to some very twisted thoughts and behaviors, like all the dangerously kinky and weird sexual stuff— the behaviors that, when you're older and get publicly exposed, puts your name in the papers and causes your wife to leave you just to keep her dignity.

The lucky boys are the ones with fathers who are not afraid of their sexuality and who teach their boys that healthy sex is one of life's greatest pleasures. These kids can get horny, go into a private space, masturbate, clean up, roll over, and go to sleep. No guilt; no conflict. As they get older, their fathers teach them about having sex with partners—which is a much more complicated issue. They learn what to do with their dicks once their sexuality starts to involve other people.

If you are (or were) not one of the lucky guys, find someone you can trust to talk with about sex., someone who will listen to you without judging you for your sexual feelings and desires. Hopefully, find a man at least ten years older than you who seems—at least, to some reasonable extent—to have his shit together.

These waters are too complex to navigate alone.

CHAPTER SIX

Getting Loaded

Any book claiming to help young guys like you grow and keep their balls has to spend some time talking about getting loaded. When men overuse and/ or abuse drugs, especially alcohol—the most common and arguably the most destructive recreational drug of all—we grow false balls; our courage isn't real and our decisions are often dumb. Sometimes, when we're unlucky, those decisions have huge and terrible consequences. This sucks, of course, because when we got loaded, we were just trying to have a good time. Nothing wrong with that, right? Right. Except, unfortunately, good intentions don't always produce good outcomes.

So guys, we have to spend some time talking about drugs. From alcohol, which is just a legal drug, to the illegal drugs you get on the street, to drugs you get from a doctor, drugs are an inescapable part of life—always have been; always will be. When it comes to drugs, the issue is not which ones are "good" and which ones are "bad," or which ones are legal and which ones are not. That is a matter of political and economic debate, if not personal taste. *Any* drug, illegal or legal, can be abused. The real issue is your *relationship* to whatever drugs you take. How you manage your relationships with them has a lot to do with how healthy you will be and how successful you will be as a man.

We're going to go back to your childhood—before you even knew what a drug was—to look at your issues with drugs, because you already knew about getting high. When you were a little kid, you quickly learned that going in circles got you dizzy and loopy; it made you feel weird—but in a good way. You log-rolled down grassy hills. You put your arms out and spun yourself in circles until you fell into the grass, flat on your back, with the world spinning crazily around you. It was cool and different. If you did it too much, you felt sick, giving you your first exposure to a universal law I'll repeat several times in this chapter: *Everything in moderation.* Too much of even a good thing is a problem.

Rolling and spinning, running in circles, breathing in and out fast and then holding your breath—what were you doing? You were getting high— pure and simple. The little kid version of getting fucked up, messing with your head. In adult terms, you were deliberately altering your brain chemistry— and with it, your perceptions and consciousness—for *the fun of it.* It was cool, and normal. Our brains *like* that sort of thing. They like being challenged and entertained, even if it means now and again being thrown off balance for a while.

You had every reason to believe this was okay behavior. The adults in your life *supported* this kind of playing. We dads love horseplay with kids. We love spinning them in circles and dangling them upside down. Your neighborhood playground probably had one of those gray metal merry-go-rounds sunk into the sand, where you and your friends spun around, holding on for dear life until you fell off (or in my case, were about to throw up). From the swings to the monkey bars, from the spinning tires suspended from chains, to the wiggly suspension bridges between play structures, everything in a playground is designed to give your brain a temporary twist on the world *because it feels good.* The rides at county fairs and theme parks do the same thing (only better, right?). *They are designed to get us high* by stimulating our brains to alter our brain chemistry, and therefore, alter our perceptions. They work on us because they are out of the ordinary and a challenge to our brains. If we rode them every day they would soon become ordinary, uninteresting, and no longer able to get us high. The best rollercoaster in the world would soon become a "so what?" experience if you rode it too much.

Anything you use to get high will lose its punch when overused. All drugs and most risky activities fit into this equation. To get back the high you like, whatever it is, requires *cutting back* from overuse. Again, the expression "Everything in moderation" applies here. Addicts are people who, for whatever reason, are unable to pull off this balancing act. Those "in recovery" have decided to stop trying. The struggle to keep their lives in balance while continuing to use substances isn't worth it. For them, just plain *not using* works much better. When you continue to use a drug even though you're no longer getting the desired benefits of the high—or are getting negative consequences—it's time to do something else, don't you think?

The other ways of getting high, the healthy ones we found as kids (activities, hobbies, and other amusements) also involve drugs. All the "high on life" methods—from laughing with friends to parachuting from airplanes—they involve drugs too. But they are our natural drugs, we produce them internally instead of taking them in from the outside, and they are part of the body's standard equipment. These "high on life" behaviors trigger the body to release its own natural protective drugs. Think about it this way: we are born with internal first aid kits, factories in our bodies that produce our own supplies of stimulants, hallucinogens, depressants, and pain-killing drugs. These are substances an organism like us needs now and then to survive. Animals have them and so do we humans. These drugs are divine gifts, if you are inclined to think in spiritual terms.

If you draw these natural, internally made drugs out chemically (think back to chemistry class), they look very similar to certain prescription and street drugs we take, looking more or less for the same physical, mental, and/or emotional effects. Chemically, they *have* to look similar or they wouldn't have the desired effect on us. Like a puzzle piece needing its exact match to fit and bring on the drug's effect, a drug works in your body only if you have the right-shaped neural receptor in your brain to receive it.

These internal "home made" drugs flood our blood streams (in exactly the right amount) when we really need them. For example, when we get *really* scared, they give us the strength and stamina to run long distances—fast—to escape danger. They are the magic responsible for giving a frail grandmother the sudden superhuman strength to yank a car off of her grandchild pinned underneath it. They create the slow-motion time warp we go into while our bodies are thrown about during a car accident. We are kept calm and pain-free for a time—even if our bodies are being badly injured.

Wild rides or risky activities like bungee jumping, skydiving, and the fast, racing sports get the body to release a good-sized dose of those brain chemicals. Until they wear off, we feel high and enjoy the effects. Other "high on life" activities do the same thing, but in smaller chemical doses. Video games seem to have this same effect on young guys.

I get high from playing my guitar or drums. Even during hours of a quiet activity, like model building or even writing, I can get a nice feeling of calm and experience timelessness—hours slipping by without my noticing. Playing golf, tennis, or shooting hoops get me high, and the effect I get is certainly pleasurable, but I'm sure it's less intense than the high my ski-racing friends get when they fly down a double black-diamond slope. And it's far less intense than a dose of cocaine or speed or a hit of LSD. On the other hand, my hobbies carry fewer risks. Anyway, when I perform (and it goes well), I'm not sure the high I get is that far behind the racers . . .

When you take recreational drugs, you have to regulate the dosage yourself, using as a guide post your past experience with the drug (if you have any) or whatever advice you can get from other people who have taken it. But they can only testify to their own experience—how it worked for *them*. This makes taking their advice somewhat dicey since what is just enough for one person is way too much for another. Anyone who has ever dabbled in substance use knows this. Men and women metabolize substances differently. Weight is a consideration, as well; it can have a strong effect on how much of a drug is safe for any given person to take.

You've seen this in your friends: Some people can't even feel a couple of beers while the same amount causes somebody else to get pretty drunk and somebody else to just fall asleep on the couch. Some people can do a few lines of cocaine and stay up all night dancing and talking (usually too much) and suffer no ill effects the next morning. Another person may snort the same amount, but having no idea he or she has a hidden heart condition, suddenly suffers a fatal heart attack. These things happen—not often, but they happen. The punch line is this: We are all wired a little differently from each other so the same drug will have different effects on different people.

You can also have big problems if your drug supply varies in quality (and most illegal drugs do). Now and again you will read in the newspaper about experienced heroin addicts dropping dead in clusters in a certain area, overdosing after years of steady and uneventful use. What usually has happened is that a batch of stronger-than-usual heroin hits the streets and by the time word gets around that the common dose is too much, several people are dead. This is true of milder drugs, as well, though fortunately with less dangerous results. For example, most marijuana is much stronger today than it used to be; the guy who hasn't smoked in years had better take it slow and easy if he decides to join in on the joint being passed around today. He may find himself feeling far higher than he had planned or anticipated; the ensuing anxiety may make him unable to enjoy himself until the effects wear off some and he starts to stabilize.

This doesn't happen with a naturally produced high. Your body knows how much of its own drug you need and it regulates your dosage accordingly. Plus, there are so many ways to get high that no matter what kind of high you like, there are always natural ways to get there. If you're used to getting loaded with outside drugs and are now switching to the natural route, your body will adjust to the available internal supply and dosage as long as you keep giving your brain reasons to produce them.

What you choose to do depends on the kind of high you want. You don't have to skateboard down a steep hill to get a natural high. Having a great and satisfying conversation releases some of those natural brain chemicals and leaves you feeling high. Skill-based activities like sports, music, dancing, and art leave you feeling high. Competition and/or performing in front of people makes the high stronger and longer lasting. Even prayer gets you high; it produces a positive physical, emotional, and mental response, no matter what your spiritual or religious beliefs are. Think about it: You've had that natural-high feeling before, haven't you?

Interestingly, these are the same "drugs" responsible for that amazing "falling in love" feeling you get at the start of a relationship. So, while love is surely real, part of its reality is chemical. All of our emotions, from anger and fear to love and joy, are expressed through our brain chemistry, which cause us to experience and interpret our feelings one way or another. Our bodies are beautiful complex machines operating in the physical world, receptive to drug stimulation from both the outside and the inside and responding to all of them by altering our moods. This is not a good or bad thing; it just is.

So, how do you learn to have a good relationship with a drug? My advice: Before experimenting with alcohol and/or whatever else looks tempting, get good at activating the natural drugs within you first. You started that as a kid. I am not making a moral judgment here. My advice is based on knowing what skills you will need to be a successful man. One skill you definitely need is being able to effectively alter your mood from a bad state of mind to a good one. Everyone gets bored and frustrated. Everyone experiences stress and anxiety. How do you break out of them and get into a better mood? As a young man, it's important that you know how to and practice doing this naturally, without any "outside" drugs at all. Otherwise, you end up *relying* on them to do the job, which puts you at their mercy. If you *need* a drug to alter your mood and it's not available, you're stuck with your mood. When young people move from satisfying their curiosity to actual "experimentation" to steady use (or abuse), they risk growing up without learning how to regulate their own moods. *That* is a problem.

As a young man, your desire to get loaded with your friends is as normal now as it was when you were a little kid playing with your buddies on the merry-go-round. The question is *how* are you going to get high? Being able to make yourself feel good is a key to your emotional (and even physical) freedom. Whether or not you choose to ever use any "outside" recreational drugs, you need to have reliable ways of making yourself feel good. You need hobbies. You need skills. Don't say that girls are your hobby—or sex—unless you are talking about masturbation (and I know you aren't; I'm not sure that qualifies as a hobby, anyhow). You need to have some hobbies that do not rely on other people. You need to be able to take care of yourself.

If you rely primarily on substances to get you off, your odds of developing a drug problem or an addiction go through the roof. The people who live successful, free lives while using drugs (legal or illegal) rely on their *sobriety* to accomplish the things important to that success and freedom.

Remember: Everything in Moderation. For example, a successful athlete knows that getting loaded can ruin his sports career. So, he either doesn't use drugs at all or only uses them in circumstances and in amounts that he thinks will be safe for his body, mind, career, and freedom. Only an uncommitted (or foolish) athlete takes risks with his future. Sure, some drug addicts have made it to the pros and become stars, but not many. Of those who have, many are now writing books and warning guys like you to not follow their examples. How many potential Michael Jordans, Joe Montanas, or Wayne Gretzkys have killed or maimed themselves in drunk-driving accidents or otherwise ruined their careers before they even got started? All by doing stupid shit while loaded. I'll bet you know a person or two who fits that category. We all do.

*   *   *

How Do I Know if I Have a Problem?

If you're going to allow yourself to use alcohol or street drugs (or engage in risky behaviors), here is a test to help you to see your risk factors and determine if you are using them responsibly. There are no specific right and wrong answers here; no special score you could get which proves that you "have a problem" or guarantees that you don't. As useful as I have found it to be, the test is just a tool for you to use. The only opinion that counts is your own. You will decide to change your behavior if *you* think you should, not because of some score on a test or because someone tells you they believe you have a problem (even if they're right). Your behavior may be too costly in my opinion, but so what? What is too hefty a price for me to pay may mean nothing to you.

I developed the following test while leading court-ordered therapy groups for men who had two or more felony convictions for driving under the influence. If you were in my group, in order to get the restrictions taken off of your driver's license, you were stuck with me and up to fourteen other guys like yourself for eighteen straight months of weekly group therapy (with testing to enforce and prove your sobriety)—so I had a captive audience on which to try this test out. According to the guys, this worked pretty well for many of them.

The party-line counseling approach among all of the group leaders at the agency (except me) was to get the clients to admit they were "alcoholics" and push them into working the twelve-step Alcoholics Anonymous program. Hopefully, this would get them to stop drinking for good. Though this treatment plan had good intentions, many of the guys did not respond well to having the ALCOHOLIC label stamped onto them; this was especially true of the younger guys. In response to this heavy-handed approach, many of them wasted their time in counseling groups. Many of these guys in my groups had been through the process before and described having spent their time in the program fighting the "ALCOHOLIC" label. And they were good at it. Like expert defense lawyers, they looked for any holes in the counselor's logic or approach that they could use to justify ignoring the most important issue being taught to them: Their *drinking* was causing them (and those around them) serious problems.

Labeling people doesn't tend to work well; very few of us like being put into categories. Nonetheless, most of my fellow counselors dutifully tried to get the clients to wear the alcoholic label, believing that this was necessary for the drunk drivers to change their behaviors. Often unable to keep up with the ensuing war of wits, the counselors, many of whom were also recovering alcoholics, fell back on the "you're in denial" approach to their argumentative clients. They had to hope that more AA meetings would break that *denial* and put these "alcoholics" on the road to recovery. In the meantime, counselors dubbed these guys "resistant" and "not ready to get sober" because they had not yet "hit bottom." The well-intentioned counselors saw their job as breaking down that denial; unfortunately, this approach set up a power struggle with the guys who weren't buying what the counselor was selling.

As a treatment approach, this made no sense to me. Alcoholics Anonymous and other twelve-step programs work great for some people but they are not the only way to help a person to change destructive behaviors. For a variety of reasons, twelve-step programs are a bad fit for many people. Seeing this firsthand, I didn't want any of my group members to fall between the cracks. Just because a guy didn't relate well to some or all of the tenets of Alcoholics Anonymous, I didn't want him to miss out on the chance to get honest with himself. Since most of these guys in the program had driven under the influence *hundreds of times*, I didn't want to waste any opportunity to have a sobering impact on them. When I led those groups, I used to think of all the victims who were dead or maimed from drunk-driver accidents. I thought of their families and friends—and the next unknown victims who would suffer if my guys went back to old behaviors after the program. The judge and I were society's last, best hope. I owed it to all of these people to do a good job at helping my guys to change their ways.

So, I thought, why get into a pissing contest over a label? I was much less interested in convincing the guys that they were alcoholics than I was in helping them to decide if *they* thought they should drink—and if so, how much? I figured these guys weren't going to change their real-life behaviors because of what *I* might say or think.

After looking at their drinking behaviors through my test, many of the group members—old, middle-aged, and young—came to the conclusion that they shouldn't drink. As one guy in his early thirties simply explained, "I stopped drinking because when I drink, I drink too much."

Ka-boom.

That, for me, was the best possible outcome for a guy most counselors would label, right or wrong, as "ALCOHOLIC." As for me, I didn't care how or if he labeled himself; I didn't even care if he stopped drinking altogether; I just cared that he stop drinking and driving. The rest was up to him. The test was designed for him to figure out for himself what kind of relationship he had with alcohol and what he intended to do about the trouble he had gotten himself into over his use of it.

The test questions that follow refer to drinking alcohol. However, if alcohol isn't your issue, feel free to substitute *any substance or behavior* that might be a problem for you: using (other) drugs, spending money unwisely, having unsafe/ unwise sex, overeating, watching too much television, spending too much time on video games or internet porn—whatever worries you about yourself. They are all ways of getting loaded. Remember, the key to success in pleasurable activities is moderation. Personal power comes from *acting on self-knowledge*. Substances (and risky behaviors), in and of themselves, are rarely the problem. It is our relationship to them that matters. So, look at your relationship with your substance (or behavior) along the following seven life domains. Again, ask the hard questions and give yourself honest answers. My test is written to help you get to know yourself better.

Test: Do I Have a Drinking Problem?

The Question: How has your use of alcohol affected:

1. your health?

Think about all ways in which your use of alcohol has affected your body. I remember one guy in his early twenties saying that until he got sober again, he couldn't remember the last time he had taken a solid shit. That's quite a realization from a normally healthy twenty-two-year-old man. Older guys have an easier time seeing the damaging effects of alcohol on their bodies than do the younger guys. They see the red, wrinkled skin and feel the long-term effects of chronic, heavy alcohol use. But the young human body is strong; it will take quite a bit of abuse and punishment before it starts sending out "you're fucking up" messages to the brain. For this reason, when considering their health, this first question, I focused the younger guys in my groups on the times when they got hurt while drunk. The car accidents (and "almost" accidents) they've been in; the times they fell down and got hurt; the stupid fights they got into while drinking. Seen like this, the health question paints with a wide brush.

If you ever got drunk and had, oh, let's call it *unwise sex* with someone you didn't know well (or at all) and ended up catching a venereal disease that counts in this question too. Consider yourself lucky if you escaped with something treatable. Even if you avoided the fatal diseases like AIDS or hepatitis C, we know that unwise/unprotected sex opens you up to a whole list of ugly diseases. If you come down with herpes simplex II, for example, are you ready to *tell all your future sexual partners* about your "little problem"? Meanwhile, if you got this girl got pregnant, there are the legal and financial issues for you to chew on. But for now, let's stick to health consequences.

How about something common: Have you kept drinking until you threw up? People laugh about this sort of thing, but consider this: When you throw up from drinking too much, you have actually poisoned yourself. You drank more alcohol than your body could safely metabolize. With a bigger job than it can handle, your brain protects itself by making you throw up the alcohol that has now become a poison to your system. Most of the time, it isn't a problem—it's more of an embarrassment. Every now and then, however, someone passes out, vomits, chokes on it, and dies. Rock stars Jim Morrison of the Doors and Janis Joplin choked to death on their vomit, too drunk and high to save themselves.

Another health issue is blacking out. Essentially, blacking out means not remembering what you did or said while you were drunk the day/night before. Now, I know that blacking out makes for funny material for comedians. It's considered funny to not remember where you parked your car or to wake up next to someone you don't know or remember screwing. But think about this: If you have *ever* blacked out from drinking, you drank *so much alcohol* that, in response, your brain actually began the process of shutting itself down for survival. Essentially, you had alcohol poisoning and if you had continued drinking, you might have died from it.

If you stress the brain with too much alcohol, it will let go of what it sees as less important functions, like reason, speech, and balance. You slur your words, your vision gets distorted and you may stumble around on your feet, even falling and hurting yourself. You make poor decisions like getting behind the wheel of a car or you may shoot off your mouth and say ugly things to people you would never have said while sober. Next to go is your memory; that's the blackout I-don't-remember-what-I-did-or-said-last-night experience.

Your brain will shut down function after function in favor of keeping you breathing and your heart beating. Keep drinking after that and your brain eventually throws in the towel . . . and you die. This happens every fall at high school parties. It happens at bars and in dorms and fraternity houses. At college, a kid turning eighteen or twenty-one gets encouraged/pushed by his (or her) friends into drinking a ton of alcohol—sometimes even eighteen or twenty-one drinks—to celebrate the big birthday. Because most bodies and brains can't handle that much alcohol that fast, the birthday boy or girl ends up dead from alcohol poisoning. We all read in the newspaper about the carloads of young people killed in drunk-driving accidents.

I know these are extreme examples. But alcohol-related deaths for young guys like you *happen all the time*. I'm not talking about twenty-year-old kids who are already serious drunks. I'm talking about regular guys who usually down a few beers and occasionally get drunk. Actually, the regular heavy drinker is less likely to die from alcohol poisoning than a guy who goes a little nuts one night and decides to *really* get hammered. A heavy drinker's body is somewhat used to getting soaked with alcohol. It's breaking down steadily, but it won't be shocked to death by a case of beer.

By the way, you do know that heavy drinking affects your ability to perform sexually, don't you? Is drinking more important than getting laid? I'm just asking . . .

2. How has your use of alcohol affected your schoolwork or career?

I don't judge any guy on his school smarts. We all have different strengths and challenges when it comes to the classroom. If you are doing your best, you have my respect, no matter what your grades are. Likewise for what a guy does for an honest day's work. I don't care what you do for a living. But if your drinking habits limit your career choices, that's a sign of a problem. Say for example you used to think you were going to be a professional of some sort—the kind that requires at least a college degree, if not a master's or PhD. You saw yourself doing something exciting like becoming a jet pilot, an astronaut, or an engineer; maybe you wanted to be a doctor, architect, or lawyer. But then you got introduced to your drug of choice and got distracted from your schoolwork. You started getting loaded too often. By the time you figured out what had happened, it was too late to get it together academically—or you didn't think you could—so you settled for a less demanding (and probably lower paying) career. Getting loaded became more important to you than your own future.

Remember: it is *your relationship* with a drug that counts. It doesn't matter if your friends drink more than you do. What matters here is your drinking behavior and its effect on your academic and/or vocational career.

The same idea holds true for you guys already in the work world, even if you are working in your chosen career. If you are in this category, ask yourself this: Has drinking interfered with your career? Do you have a reputation as a heavy drinker? Have you ever missed work from being hung over? Have you embarrassed yourself at work? Has your partying ever gotten you fired? Think about it. What seemed like harmless fun, telling funny drinking stories around work, may have had bad consequences. Co-workers may have laughed along with you or even told their own stories. But drinking stories get around and heavy drinking makes people nervous. It does *not* inspire confidence. Since bosses are responsible for how their people produce and perform, they are less likely to promote the guy with all the funny Monday-morning drinking stories, even if he has seniority. Also, many a boss has been told off by a snot-drunk employee at the holiday office party who subsequently had his career cut short or squashed as a result. *People remember the stupid things we say and do when we are drunk.*

So here's a quick piece of advice: At work functions, if you drink alcohol, only drink if the boss drinks—and then, don't drink very much.

3.   How has your use of alcohol affected your finances?

This category is pretty self-explanatory. We're talking about wasted money here: paying for your alcohol (count any amount over moderation), buying expensive rounds at the bar for other people when you can't really afford it, paying to fix your car when you wreck it, paying higher insurance rates, making restitution to others for things you broke and other property damage, paying for injuries you caused, and replacing items you lost. Think about lawyer fees, fines, doctors, and dentists bills.

If you've already been married and divorced, did your drinking contribute to the breakup? If so, you need to factor in those costs: the alimony or the loss of half your hard-earned assets like a house, your other belongings, and your money.

Ever get a drunken one-night stand pregnant? Remember, *she* gets to choose if she has an abortion or keeps the child. Like it or not, fair or not, you're just the interested bystander. If she chooses door number two, you're in for at least eighteen years of child support—never mind all the other duties and responsibilities of a good father.

Be honest about the money angle here and you'll come up with a much better and more complete list of examples for yourself than I can. When you've done that, assign some round but honest dollar amounts to the items on the list and add them up. Make sure you're sitting down when you hit the equal sign. Most people with alcohol problems are afraid to make this list because the truth is ugly and painful.

4.   How has your use of alcohol affected your legal issues?

Hopefully, there is nothing for you to consider here. But there certainly was for all the guys in my drinking-driver groups. Anytime your recreational behaviors get you into legal troubles, from fathering unplanned children to getting caught breaking laws, you know you have some problems to consider.

Have you ever been arrested or seen the inside of a jail cell, even for a few hours, because of your drinking? That is *not* normal. Ask around. Most people have not had that experience. If that's a common experience among the people you hang around with, try asking yourself: "Who the hell are my friends?"

If your drinking has led to legal problems relating to violence, especially violence against women, you really have problems. I know this sounds like therapy talk, but the truth is you probably have some serious unresolved childhood issues that need your attention. If you are only violent or mean to women when you drink, what does that tell you about yourself? Does even thinking about this make you want to drink? Hold on, because the next question is all about your relationships.

5. How has your use of alcohol affected your relationships?

Whole books are written on this one. Start with your parents and the rest of your immediate family. How are or were your relationships with them affected by your drinking? If you come from a family where heavy drinking or other substance abuse was common, this becomes a complicated question because *your family's* behavior affected their relationships with *you*. It was not fair that you did not get good role modeling in this area, but frankly, life isn't fair. You know that. So, it's up to each of us to either continue the family tradition or go in a healthier direction of our own choosing.

Now that you've given some thought to what we therapists call your "family of origin"—the folks you grew up with—think about other people close to you: your friends, girlfriends, your wife (or wives). Think about your children, if you have them. Think about colleagues and bosses. If you're still in school, think about teachers or coaches. What have these people said about your behaviors or your sense of responsibility? How are their observations or remarks related to your drinking?

Have you blown it while drinking (for example, made mistakes you later regret) and then made deals with yourself or others to stop drinking or slow down, only to later on break that agreement? This is pretty common. If it's true of you, instead of bargaining with these people for some slack around your drinking, think about why you drink. Have you lost close relationships because people don't want to be around you when you drink? Do you tend to avoid socializing with people who don't drink? Be honest with yourself. Do you feel *entitled* to drink? Why do you feel cheated if you are not getting loaded? Does it feel unfair when people complain about your drinking? Why?

The probable answer: You have some unmet emotional needs and you use heavy drinking as a Band-Aid. For deep wounds, Band-Aids only help a little and for just a while. If these questions are hitting home for you it is not because you are a bad guy. You are having these troubles because you are not using the other skills you need to take care of yourself. You're expecting alcohol to meet (or mask) your emotional needs, not to enhance your life as it can by many people when used in moderation.

If people say you are significantly *different* when you drink (you become an asshole, for example), this is a sign of a drinking problem. True, moderate amounts of alcohol have a mild changing effect to our personalities. We loosen up a little and become less self-conscious—maybe a little braver, socially, than usual. After a drink or two, we may get up the nerve to walk up and speak to the girl or woman we want to meet. As effects of light to moderate drinking, these are all okay. They are, for the most part, the reason people drink in the first place. This is not the same as getting loaded and turning mean. No one drinks in order to become an asshole. But if that is what happens when you drink, how do you feel about it and what do you think it means? Also, you need to be able to meet and talk to a woman without a drink in your hand, you know.

Again, forgive me the therapy talk, but if you have this sort of personality change when you drink, there is a problem—not just your drinking but with something inside you which you avoid looking at. Whatever it is, even though you try and ignore it, it affects you and your relationships anyway. When you drink and loosen up, instead of getting friendly and maybe a little relaxed and brave, a cage gets opened and a beast bearing your face appears. You better have a look at it before it leaves you lonely or buries you.

These relationship questions are all pretty important, so be honest with yourself when you answer them. If you don't like the answers you're coming up with then drinking has clearly become too important to you and your relationship with alcohol is not healthy. It's important that you sort this out because people are probably already wondering if being around you is worth it.

6.   How has your use of alcohol affected your self-esteem?

This one is easy. It is about inner conflict and how you feel about yourself. You should already know this answer. This category is about you feeling guilty, worried, or ashamed about your drinking. It is about making deals with yourself (or God or another person) and then dropping the ball.

Have you tried to control your drinking but failed? Typically, a guy trying to control a drinking problem will set up rules for himself that, if he follows them, will make sure he drinks in moderation. If he can follow the rules, he will look like a normal drinker, the kind whose alcohol use does not get him into any trouble. Unfortunately, some people can't pull this off. If you are one of them, you may start out the evening planning to follow your own rules, but despite your good intentions, you drink right past moderation and slide into drunkenness. At this point, alcohol affects your good (sober) decision-making abilities.

Living life through this scenario is a sign of a drinking problem.

Have you switched types of alcohol to try and make yourself drink less? Have you promised yourself that you would stop drinking—only to start again when you felt better? These things are common in people with substance abuse problems.

We lose respect for ourselves when we make promises and then break them. This makes us feel bad, which in turn makes us want to drink to "forget." And the cycle continues . . .

7. Last question: How has your use of alcohol affected your emotions?

We men *do* have feelings. Because our behavior is often driven more by our heads than our hearts (including the little head), women accuse us of not having any feelings. You know this isn't true. But our culture teaches a boy that expressing his real feelings makes him vulnerable and will be seen as a sign of weakness. So he bottles them up until they come out in weird ways, often while he's drinking.

So, how do you handle your feelings? What do you do when you get bored? How about nervous (or downright scared)? How do you handle sadness or grief? What about frustration or anger? What do you do to feel better? Is one of the answers "I get loaded"? Is that one of your main ways of feeling better?

Your ways of handling your emotions has a lot to do with how you were raised. If your family had unhealthy ways of handling feelings, you picked up those too, just from watching, since our family members are our first role models. Sometimes we avoid our parents' particular bad habits only to go too far in some bad habit of our own choosing. However, if you look around, you'll notice that there are other, more balanced ways of responding to difficult feelings. Other people act differently than our families did. You have probably already figured out that developing healthy ways of handling emotions does take some hard work, however. The old ways come back easy though, so be careful.

So, that's it. That's the test—seven areas for you to consider when it comes to your behaviors that may worry you. As you can see, there are no scores to add up. There may be several areas in which you are "doing just fine" while one or two more have you a little concerned. That's good. The whole idea is to think clearly and be honest with yourself. What you choose to do with your own answers is up to you.

So, do you think you have a problem or are you perhaps headed toward one? What did you decide? If you feel comfortable with your life as it is, that's great. That's the answer you wanted, right? You can use the test to monitor yourself over time as you continue to use substances. Remember: Everything in moderation.

On the other hand, if you're not feeling so confident about your use of substances after reading the test, or if you have actually decided that you do have a problem, then it is up to you to seek a solution. Help is out there, from individual and group counseling to Alcoholics Anonymous and other such groups that work great for some people. But you have to ask for it.

*　　*　　*

Big reminder for teenagers (or anyone who started using substances early):

As we covered earlier, the big problem with you getting loaded at this age is that it keeps you from developing your own emotional survival skills. If you started getting loaded as a boy or teenager, unless you have since stopped using, you are probably not so good at dealing with your feelings. We all have to learn to take care of ourselves: it is called self-soothing. This is a skill you need to avoid being dependent on other things or people to make yourself feel okay when you get stressed. I strongly urge young people not to use alcohol and other drugs because it is too easy to become dependent on them.

When we're boys, our parents are *supposed* to soothe our social bumps and bruises. One of their jobs, besides keeping us fed, clothed, and safe, is to teach us how to get along with other people and how to deal with the feelings we stumble across in everyday life. By coaching and guiding us through our little social lives—and the different feelings they bring—our parents soothe our hurt feelings. They teach the lessons that prepare us to make good decisions in life, like who to trust and how to choose friends. Good parents also model other self-soothing skills—things you can do alone—so you don't have to rely so much on other people, things like hobbies, sports, or reading for pleasure.

As you've grown from boy to teenager, your needs have changed. As a teenager, you now may need your parents to back off some and let you learn how to make your own decisions. You need to find your way through bad feelings. Your parents can help, of course. So can friends, teachers, relatives, and coaches—anyone you trust. But there's no substitute for learning skills for how to make yourself feel better.

What follows are discussions on three skills you need to be able to take care of yourself. Having them will help keep you moderate with your substance use, should you choose to use at all, and will help you to feel like a man with Personal Power:

Positive self-talk. This is internal coaching. Hopefully, this voice is one (or a blend) of the positive adults in your life who has encouraged you all along. Positive self-coaching is a skill missing in many a man today. Unfortunately, the coaching voice many of us find in our heads is some abusive maniac from our past telling us we'll never amount to anything. With an asshole like this in your head, getting loaded to shut him up makes sense. Unfortunately, in the long run, heavy drinking tends to make you just like him and *you* end up the asshole in someone else's head—like your own son's. With positive self-talk in your bag of tricks, you can practice self-forgiveness at those times when you make mistakes. This is another *huge* skill. Beating up on yourself when you do something stupid rarely does you much good.

Patience. One big problem with drugs is that they are so reliable. Alcohol produces its effect every time you drink it, and the waiting period is only a few minutes. *Getting loaded requires no skill.* When you medicate your bad feelings with alcohol (or any other drug), you don't learn how to handle the situation that produced the bad feeling in the first place. That sort of work takes time and effort, so not having patience becomes a problem all its own. It is like trying to fix an engine without the right tools.

Delay of gratification. Like the patience issue, being able to wait for life's goodies is vital to learning any other real skill.

Having skills makes a guy feel proud. Take, for example, a skill like guitar playing. To enjoy its benefits (like self-soothing and self-expression, not to mention attracting girls), you have to sit down and actually learn to play. This takes time, mostly, plus patience—an ability to delay gratification means lots of positive self-talk.

At the beginning, you have to deal with some annoying negatives like sore, clumsy fingers that don't do what you're trying to make them do, plus lots of complex information to learn and remember. You have to deal with sounding crummy for a while. Once you get past the initial stages of learning and clumsiness, however, you start to have some success, and with that, some real fun. At this point, you're becoming a *player,* and that feels great. The more you play, the better you get. You can have a bad day at school or work, come home, pick up your guitar and play a few songs that feel right, and end up in a much better mood. If you want, you can start writing tunes, form or join a band. This is just about impossible to accomplish if you're busy getting drunk all the time. Learning to play an instrument is hard enough when you're sober.

Adults who have learned these three skills (positive self-talk, patience, and delay of gratification) can usually use substances *moderately* to enhance their experience of life. As we have discussed in previous chapters, it is the difference between want and need that matters in your relationship with a person or a substance. When you can demonstrate to yourself and others the ability to handle your feelings while sober, you're more likely able to successfully use substances in moderation. You will use when you *want* to, not because you *need* to. There is nothing wrong with wanting the benefits of moderate use. However, when you *need* substances to feel better, you are left weak and helpless without them. Stress will unbalance you until you can get loaded again. Situations that cause us to feel upset or unbalanced in our lives *remain unchanged* while we are busy getting loaded to feel better.

A few rules to remember about getting high:

Rule No. 1: Work to maintain balance in your body, mind, and spirit. When you lose that sense of balance by abusing drugs, pay attention to and *do something about it.*

Rule No.2: Have a few sober activities that deliver a *reliable, natural high.* There are no exceptions to this rule—not even for people who successfully use drugs.

Rule No. 3: If you use drugs, legal or not, use them in moderation and make the risks you take your own. Don't put other people at risk because you are getting high.

Rule No. 4: Be ruthlessly honest with yourself about your drug use.

Rule No. 5: When people who care about you talk about your drug use, *listen*.

Follow these rules and your life will have plenty of highs. You won't have to worry about whether or not to get loaded. You will know if you can use drugs in moderation or if you are the kind of guy who is better off sticking to the internal drugs.

CHAPTER SEVEN

The Intimacy Question

Okay, let's recap what we've done so far: We're finding our balls and figuring out how to keep them; we've looked at sex and drugs. We're facing up to issues of personal integrity and learning to be accountable for what we say and do. Having taken a look at some of the responsibilities of marriage and fatherhood, we're thinking long and hard about not getting over-involved with girls and women when we are not ready for a committed relationship. So far, so good? Meanwhile, in your relationships with girls and women, you are (or will be) faced with questions and challenges about your willingness (and even your ability) to be *intimate*. You need to know how to answer those questions and challenges at this stage in your life.

Intimacy is one of those words that get thrown around when people talk about relationships and it means different things to different people. Sometimes people are talking about sex when they refer to intimacy. I'm not. Let's consult Webster's again and see what he has to say about intimacy. Webster's says intimacy is a "close, familiar, and usually affectionate relationship with another person or group." In an intimate relationship, sex may be part of the picture, but it's not the part we need to talk about.

The intimacy Worthwhile Women (and mature men/guys with balls) want can turn quickly into commitment; it is, after all, a wonderful stage in the development of a relationship. However, since we are hoping to avoid getting into "too early" commitments, you really have no excuse for not tackling this intimacy issue head-on. So, let's spend a few pages talking about intimacy. This isn't a common topic for guys to discuss but you'll soon see why you need to be familiar with the concept. Word has it that we guys are too afraid of intimacy to commit ourselves to women. Is that so?

To help illustrate a few important points in this chapter, we're going to indulge in some stereotyping—which is always a risky venture. Why? Stereotypes aren't pretty, and people generally don't like them. Here are some problems with stereotypes:

1. People getting stereotyped usually feel misunderstood (and pissed off) because their individuality gets lost in the stereotype.
2. Stereotypes are basically unfair; whatever truth they hold only goes so far.
3. Stereotypes ignore context. They have their beginnings wrapped up in historical circumstances that are usually ignored or forgotten.
4. People who stereotype others are usually close-minded, ignorant, or mean.
5. The painful kicker: Stereotypes persist because they hold some grains of truth.

So, given those pitfalls, why use stereotypes to make a point? I'm going after those grains of truth and hoping they will turn out to be golden nuggets of wisdom. When we look past the unfairness of a stereotype, we get a chance to look at an old problem in a new way. So, that said and mindful of the risks involved, let's get going with a full-blooded stereotype about women and their view of men as being afraid of intimacy and commitment.

We've all heard women complain about men's "fear of intimacy." On TV talk shows, you hear how "in touch" women are with their feelings (a stereotype)—and how *out of touch* we men are with ours (another stereotype). Supposedly, since we don't know what to do with our feelings, we men act cool, pretending that nothing bothers us. We have countless ways of avoiding our feelings, they say. We keep them at a distance out of fear of being in a "real relationship" with them where real feelings would be unavoidable. Guys, this is a pitiful load of crap.

We've heard this nonsense so often that many of us have come to believe it's true. Actually, it's an easy mistake to make because it *is* generally true that women are more *focused* on their feelings than men are. Men know this, and in mid-battle with their girlfriends or wives over "expressing feelings," sometimes figure, "Hey, maybe she's right. Maybe I am keeping her at arm's length out of a fear of intimacy."

Praise to the brave man for considering this notion but pity the foolish one who makes the mistake of pondering this possibility out loud in front of the wrong woman, the kind who picks up that ball and runs with it. Now fully validated in her "men are afraid of intimacy" theory, she'll slap the "immature" label on her man like hot fudge on ice cream and then chow down in angry self-pity at the sorry state of men today. As for her man, now fully confused and frustrated, he heads off to fix the situation by buying her whatever his guilt tells him he can afford, from flowers to diamonds. Or he says, "Fuck it, what's the use?" and heads off to get loaded.

As it turns out, he actually has other, healthier options that keep his balls intact.

What do you say we pull back the covers on a few old myths, eh? Maybe burst a few old bubbles? First, let's revisit the maturity issue for a moment, and then we'll address this tired stereotype that men are afraid of intimacy.

As we have covered previously, maturity is the result of a process; it can't be forced or rushed. A lack of maturity is natural and need not be a source of shame for any young man. Maturity requires experience, and experience comes mostly from taking risks. Since risk-taking behaviors vary from boy to boy and man to man, everyone will mature at different speeds. If this weren't true, you would see no differences in maturity between people of the same age, but you do—everyone is different. Second, there is not one clear state of maturity that everyone eventually reaches. Surprisingly, some people demonstrate great maturity at a young age while others never seem to grow up no matter how old they get. Most of us, as we grow up, are somewhere in the middle.

So, when a frustrated woman brands her guy as immature and afraid of intimacy and believes these are the reasons why he's afraid of a commitment to her, she is partly right. But so what? With a bottle of immature wine and a taste for the grapes, you have three choices: drink it as it is, put it away and wait for it to age properly, or go get something else to drink. She's trying to invent option number four but there isn't one.

Here's what our frustrated gal doesn't see: By whining about her immature guy, she's looking into a mirror but doesn't recognize the face staring back at her. You see, the intimacy problem isn't his, it's *hers*. Why? Check it out. Here's what we *do* know about intimacy:

1. Men and women *share* a limited capacity for intimacy.
2. Man or woman, your capacity for intimacy depends on:

   a. your willingness to take a chance and be vulnerable to someone else,
   b. your ability to protect yourself emotionally,
   c. your belief in your ability to recover from loss or betrayal.

3. Age and even maturity do not necessarily increase your capacity for intimacy

Let's take these one at a time.

Number one: Men and women share a limited capacity for intimacy. The girl or woman who complains that her boyfriend is afraid of intimacy and commitment is demonstrating her own limited abilities in this area. Think about it: If she were able to handle deeper intimacy, she would be attracted to a guy who could give it to her. But she isn't. She's hot for the guy whose limited capacity for intimacy matches her own, and then she complains about him for being himself. One reason a guy feels comfortable with a girl or woman in the first place is the sense that her desire for intimacy seems to more or less match his own; at some point that assumption turns out to be false.

Truthfully, a man only has an intimacy problem if:

1. he wants more intimacy than he can handle or attract, or
2. he wants to meet his partner's desires for intimacy but can't.

If *he* feels the problem is his, he can do any number of things to change, from talking about it with someone he trusts, to reading a self-help book, to going into therapy. Otherwise, however, once his girlfriend asks for what she wants in terms of closeness and intimacy, she is well advised to back off and let him respond. If she's not happy with what she hears and gets, there's no sense in badgering him to change. If she is ready for more intimacy than he can give her (he's not ready or wanting to change), she should move on to someone else.

(**Note:** Intimacy problems in a marriage are a different story altogether. Marriage is all about commitment—remember the vows?—so couples shouldn't just give up when the intimacy between them shifts. *All* couples occasionally get out of synch. This is normal and *not* a sign of a bad marriage. It *is* the sign of a marriage needing attention. Each partner continues to mature and grows, emotionally, at his or her own speed. Because of that, a person's needs change periodically. Intimacy-wise, then, you have to expect these times when you and your partner aren't clicking like you did when you got together. This is the time to rebalance the relationship, not to give it up. Instead, you renegotiate the terms of the relationship, taking into account the changes that caused the new problems to show up in the first place. You only give up your marriage if your partner can't or won't do the necessary work to fix it and the situation, as it is (and is going to stay), is something you don't want to tolerate for the rest of your life. This is why the "Happily Ever After" fairy tales about marriage are all wide-eyed bullshit. People in successful marriages always talk about how much work it takes. This is yet another reason why I encourage you to slow down and not jump too fast into a commitment.)

How can such otherwise intelligent women be so convinced that they are the ones capable of intimacy and their men are not? What's going on? Again, it's the mirror thing. She doesn't recognize the face staring back at her because she doesn't know herself as well as she thinks she does.

Usually, (warning: stereotype ahead) a woman who complains about the intimacy issue with her boyfriend(s) or husband(s) grew up disappointed with her relationship with her father. At best, he was emotionally unavailable, the sort of man with whom it's hard to connect in a meaningful way. At worst, he was emotionally, physically, or sexually abusive. For most of these women, the father/daughter relationship was in a vast gray area in between emotional distance and outright abuse.

Whatever the father-daughter formula was, the daughter walks into adulthood with her own limited experience of healthy male intimacy. As a result, she looks for a partner to match her own capacity for emotional closeness—for intimacy. I'm not saying she thinks this through consciously. She doesn't. But her "search" for a partner follows what interests her in a man. In real terms, this means: Who is she attracted to versus who bores her? This kind of woman may believe she can handle an emotionally available man, but in truth, she can't. If she could, she would attract and have one. These women often say there aren't enough mature men to go around, and maybe that's true. But a woman who can handle intimacy will attract a man (with balls) who can match her. There are lots of guys swinging around a full set of *cohones*, and a Worthwhile Woman won't settle for less in a partner. However, for the rest of the women out there, here's my question: Would you be attracted to an emotionally available man if you met him?

For many women, the answer is no, especially the kind of woman who whines about immature men. She *rejects* the guys who are emotionally available men, the Nice Guys who would treat her well (perhaps too well). She finds them *boring*. Why? She's hot for guys her own speed: the distant, emotionally unexpressive guys, maybe even Bad Boys. After all, they're pretty safe for her; she can bitch about their limitations—their "fears of intimacy"—but they won't face her with her own. This makes them a pretty good match. Of course, this isn't the woman she sees in the mirror. When she looks in the mirror, she sees a victim who's stuck with an immature guy.

There is another possibility at play here for this kind of woman—and we have to keep this idea just between you and me because its really not a popular one—but isn't it possible that while picking out her guy, she's gotten a little lost by focusing on our other qualities, like how much money we make, the kind of car we drive, our social status, or our looks? Think that's possible? It *would* be pretty shallow, though. I mean, aren't *we* the shallow ones who are known to choose our women by bra size?

Remember, we've been talking about stereotypes here, not all women. The Worthwhile Woman you want for a partner will be interested in you for your sense of humor, creativity, intelligence, and strength of character. Worthwhile Women are, by definition, pretty capable of intimacy. But remember, in terms of the future, even a marriage with her will get out of synch now and then and need retooling.

Number Two: Intimacy requires vulnerability. It means trusting another person to be a safe caretaker of your private self. In order to have emotional intimacy, you have to be willing to open up to the other person. This means sharing some parts of yourself that others, with whom you are *not* intimate, will *never* know. Face it, guys, this isn't easy. It requires a lot of trust—and since most of us have been burned at one time or another, trust doesn't come easily. Burns *hurt* and heal slowly. They leave scars.

When it comes to relationships, what happens when your intimacy is betrayed? Couples break up all the time, and it usually isn't pretty. For every friendly breakup, there are a hundred painful ones where someone ends up feeling screwed over. The details leading up to the breakup can be ugly too. People cheat on one another—sometimes with their partner's best friend. Big lies are told and promises, once sincerely made, get broken. Partners betray confidences all the time.

When this happens, the person feeling betrayed is usually not in any particular hurry to get intimate with someone else. This is a strength, however, a *good* thing; it's only smart to back off, figure out what went wrong, and heal before starting in with someone else. Frankly, you have to watch out for the other kind of person; the kind who jump right into a new relationship often end up being more trouble than they are worth. When you hear people refer to someone being "on the rebound," that's what they're talking about. This person is coming out of a relationship like a basketball careening off the boards. Rebound relationships can be intense and sexy but they often go down the tubes. The excitement of a heavy dose of the "love drug" eases the pain of the breakup, and for a while, things are wild. But when the first rush wears off and reality sets back in, the unresolved issues come right back. Not having learned anything from the last relationship (or the several before that), this kind of person has one bad and painful relationship after another without a clue as to what she is doing wrong.

Relationship hint: If you're on the rebound and you're not figuring out your contribution to the end of your last relationship, your next one is probably toast even before it gets started. You have to do your homework before you take the plunge again if you want better results next time. The same is true for your next partner. Before you sign up for a new relationship find out what happened in her last one. If she either doesn't have a clue, or isn't bothering to figure it out, or says the break-up was all *his* fault, save yourself a lot of trouble, get out while the going's easy. This will be hard because this type of woman (stereotype ahead) can be passionate and great in bed. She's knows how to catch a man; she just doesn't know what to do with him once she's got him. That kind of sex always comes with a price and unplanned pregnancies can become part of the mix. Unable to keep a man by having a good relationship, she can keep him around by having his baby. You've been warned.

What's true for nations (Those who ignore the lessons of history are doomed to repeat them.) is also true for individuals. As obvious as this is, time after time, people (and nations) do just that. We don't look honestly in the mirror. We don't ask for honest feedback from those people who know us and who watched us blunder through our last relationship. Instead, we blame the last partner for being "nuts" and we go searching for the next partner with whom to repeat the whole drama yet again. Who's the nut here?

After a breakup, steer clear of relationships for a while. New intimacy just won't feel safe until you trust your judgment again. So take a little break. Keep it light with women or maybe hold off on dating altogether for a while. This is not a matter of being afraid of intimacy. It is all about admitting that you are not ready for more right now.

Try hanging out more with your guy friends. Work on a project where you can build some skills. Accomplish something. Do some thinking. But that's not all. Before you take the plunge into an intimate relationship again, get some honest feedback from someone who knows you really well, especially if your girl left you. She may have done the obvious bad stuff like cheating or lying, so you may feel like it was all her fault and *you are* the victim. But remember, *you* chose *her*. This means her capacity for intimacy just about matched your own. You went for someone who ended up lying or cheating. What does that tell you? What red flags did you miss or ignore? In the end, it doesn't really matter what either of you did, good or bad. What matters is what you learned about *yourself* as a result of being with her. As a marriage and family therapist, I have worked with countless people who have been "betrayed" by a spouse or lover. The people who move on to happier relationships are the ones who take a timeout to do this painful work of looking honestly in the mirror and getting real feedback to think about.

*　　*　　*

Intimacy and Trust

Figuring out whom you can trust and whom you can't is a huge challenge for all young people. It's tough, because despite all the mistakes you're going to make as a young man, you still have to learn to trust your own judgment. Truthfully, you'll make errors in judgment even *after* you have matured. We all do. Because of this, we all have to be able to forgive ourselves for our mistakes and be willing to try again, hopefully, ever wiser each time. If you think of it that way, the people who burn us really end up being our teachers. They give us the experiences we need to mature and become capable of allowing intimacy into our relationships.

People raised in relatively stable families (there's really no such thing as a *normal* family, is there?) know that real intimacy is possible because they have been around it. They have felt it within their families. They have seen their parents talking and sharing feelings in a loving relationship with one another. The have watched their parents have intimacy with their friends. When kids from these "healthy" families get burned by a relationship, they are jolted from the experience like everyone else. They have to lick their wounds for a while, but they learn from the experience and recover. Kids from healthy families are used to having someone they can talk to and aren't afraid to ask for help. When they feel strong and venture out again, they begin choosing their intimate friends and partners more carefully. They get intimate again, but maybe a little more cautiously. Over time, their skills in reading people grow, and they relax a little more.

People from less healthy, more chaotic families have a much tougher time with intimacy. In families where people have severe emotional problems, mental illnesses and/or drug and alcohol problems, family intimacy takes on a much different flavor. It is hard to know whom to trust when the people you think you know seem to change so suddenly and often. There is no consistency. One moment you're treated well and you feel safe; the next, you're treated badly and you feel vulnerable. This is crazy-making. In a healthy family, there is consistency in the ways people treat one another. You may not get your way on one issue or another, but in general, your needs are noticed and efforts are made to meet them.

In less healthy families, your needs are *not* noticed, or if they are, few or inconsistent efforts are made to meet them. Unfortunately, kids from these families get used to this craziness, and without realizing it, come to expect the same in their adult relationships. So, if you're from such a family, even when you find a relatively safe partner, you can't enjoy the benefits of your good choice. Why? You want to trust the good feelings and treasure the happy moments, but all the while part of you is waiting for the other shoe to drop. You and this new partner are mismatched in terms of intimacy.

On a practical, day-today level, this is a real problem for a couple. The person from the less-healthy family can't relax substance abuse problems and trust problems are common. The better things go, the more nervous you feel. You *expect* your partner to start acting crazy (after all, everyone else you have ever been close to has), and you're nervous as hell until they do. Sometimes, (unconsciously) just to relieve the anxiety, you get the show on the road by creating a problem where there is none. You pick a fight for no good reason. Why? The ensuing chaos at least feels familiar; you know what is going on and the distance that gets created actually feels kind of good. Your partner, meanwhile, wonders what the hell they've gotten themselves into and ends up leaving you. In the end, you get what you expected to get out of the relationship.

While this painful description can be true of guys, it is much more common among women who, when raised like this, don't have much of a chance to become "Worthwhile" unless and until they get some professional help through counseling. Since we tend to go after people who share our own limited capacity for intimacy, their sometimes crazy patterns will clash with our own and end up causing amazing highs and devastating lows. This pattern is addictive and exhausting.

To break free of the emotional baggage of how you were raised and to be able to share feelings with another person—to have intimacy with them—you have to do the necessary inner-work. A good therapist can help with this. Unfortunately, there's no pill to do it for you, but the high you get from breaking free of old patterns beats any drug high I've ever had. I'm serious. Why? It means not having to be lonely anymore.

The family in which real abuse takes place has the same patterns, but much worse. They often produce kids with major intimacy and trust problems, and the kids are lucky if that's the worst of it. Abusers have their own histories of untreated trauma, usually serious, extensive childhood experiences with abuse and violence. With no healthy emotional role models around them, they grow up to pass on their own screwed up sense of intimacy to everyone else in the household.

Kids from these families have it *very* tough. The ones who end up emotionally healthy somehow learn to protect themselves, usually through the attention of one or a few healthy people who help them figure out how to decide whom they can and cannot trust. They learn when to put up extra strong walls between themselves and the more dangerous people in their lives. These wonderful folks are literally lifesavers. They may be neighbors, friends, or relatives; sometimes, a very wise and generous teacher or coach plays this role. They showed that a healthier way of relating to yourself and to other people was possible. The kids without that special mentoring often go on to abuse the next generation of kids, continuing the tragic cycle and keeping social workers and therapists in business.

Maybe now you can see why I'm a little touchy about this intimacy issue. It isn't fair to just accuse someone of being immature or afraid of intimacy. When it comes to intimacy, the real question is, "*How safe do you feel being vulnerable to another person?*" Sharing your thoughts and feelings with someone else does make you vulnerable to getting those feelings ignored or hurt, at the very least; and at the worst, betrayed.

No matter what sort of environment you are raised in, you have your own comfort zone when it comes to intimacy and when that comfort zone is threatened, you're going to pull back and put up some barriers to feel safe. Your method may not be so healthy (getting loaded) or you may overreact (like squirrel hunting with a bazooka) but somehow, you're going to emotionally protect yourself.

So, to sum up this intimacy issue, are we talking about a fear of intimacy or the natural behavior of someone on a growth curve? I say the latter. If you see yourself behaving in any of these self-protective patterns, it isn't because you're a man; it's about how you were raised. Fear of intimacy does exist, but it has nothing to do with gender.

Meanwhile, *everyone* gets emotional wounds growing up and has some bad memories. Everyone gets burned; that's unavoidable. Sometimes, new relationships bring up bad memories or fears, and an old wound we thought was healed reopens. We get a short fuse for a while and get told we're acting strange. We pull back from intimacy for a while. When this happens to you, calm down and catch your breath. Your comfort zone has been breeched and you need some time to heal (again) and gain some insight into what is happening now and why it brings up what happened in the past. You need some space to work through these feelings. If this happens for your girlfriend or wife, she needs some space too. We all get out of balance now and then.

Unfortunately, some people are not patient enough to let this happen at their partner's own pace, perhaps because this pull-back time kicks off their own fears and insecurities. In response, they push for more involvement and intimacy from the wounded one who is not yet ready for it. This is a mistake and can doom the relationship. Now you have *two* wounded people in the relationship. Great, huh?

Again, we get what we expect to get out of a relationship. If you expect your partner to always be there to make you feel better, no matter how he or she may be feeling at the moment, you're guaranteed to get disappointed. It seems pretty unfair to accuse somebody in this position of being afraid of intimacy, don't you think?

Figuring out how you got into such a relationship jam is sometimes painful. Some people even steer clear of the ups and downs of intimate relationships *by avoiding them altogether*. Read this carefully: **There is nothing wrong with making this choice.**

You've met people like this; people who have decided not to get into intimate relationships. Pursuing them for more than friendship is a waste of time, and at some point, if they've made their choice clear, even disrespectful. If you're really attracted to someone like this, what are you seeing when *you* look in the mirror? They are making a clear choice based on self-knowledge. What are you doing?

Leave them alone. If and when they get lonely enough, they may give intimacy another try. Or they won't. It is not up to you or me to judge how much intimacy another person should have. If you keep knocking on a closed door, it says more about you than it does the person on the other side.

Meanwhile, don't confuse intimacy with sex. Intimacy and sexuality are wonderful together. That's what we folks in long-term relationships have to replace the fireworks of sex with new partners. But people often think that intimacy and sexuality automatically go hand in hand. That is simply not the case. Both men and women can have sex with people they barely know, and although their two bodies will be close and therefore somewhat intimate, there may be no emotional intimacy at all. This kind of sex may fulfill a sexual hunger or fantasy, and depending on your own morals and values, be fine in and of itself. Or it may be all the intimacy that person can handle. If you expect real intimacy to come out of a relationship that started out sexually, you are probably fooling yourself; you're no more ready for that kind of intimacy than is your partner.

Finally, number three: Age and maturity do not necessarily increase your ability to be intimate with another person. All people have their limits when it comes to intimacy. If you want to increase your ability to be intimate, you need to understand why you have set up your defenses as you have. Once you've done that, you can decide if you still need those defenses as they are or if you can, as a maturing person, modify them. The person you are becoming may not need such a strong defense.

It is best to pay attention to these issues while you are young and strong. It's a big project to take on midway through life and the reason some people never do the work. They fall back on clichés like, "You can't teach on old dog new tricks."

* * *

Intimacy and Parenting

The issue of deciding whether or not to be a parent comes into play here. I have heard many people say they have decided not to have children because they are too selfish. I never try and talk them out of this position. Instead, I applaud them and respect their decision. Such a statement is a demonstration of great self-knowledge and maturity. Everyone has a right to be happy. If the challenges of parenting are not what you think you want, then by all means, find your joy doing something else. There is plenty of good you can offer the world without adding to its population. Being a good parent is a *huge* commitment and many people who take that road are not ready for the journey.

Children are the very definition of needy. Their needs for consistent intimacy are tremendous and no one should take on the job unless they are ready to devote, selflessly, huge amounts of emotional investment, time, effort, and money to the job well. If more people were honest with themselves about this, far fewer children would be born, and those that were would be better taken care of. But that is not what's happening. Depressed young girls look for happiness in motherhood—which almost never works—while society still puts pressure on young people to marry and have children, as though no other lifestyle can be fulfilling. This means job security for social workers and therapists, but if this situation could change for the better, I, for one, would be happy to find something else to do for a living.

CHAPTER EIGHT

So, You're in Love...

I believe in love. And yet that simple declaration is the only easy thing I have to say about it. When it comes to commenting on love relationships, especially for people your age, saying anything else feels like riding a pogo stick through a minefield. Love relationships are not simple matters, and all too often, what feels healthy and *so right* at the moment doesn't turn out to be so in the long run. Our feelings can betray us, unfortunately; so, having a little balance between head and heart is a good thing. If you're "in love" and trying to figure out if your relationship is healthy or you're wondering if you're even ready to be in a relationship, here are a few pointers from someone objective, someone without any other agenda other than keeping you out of trouble.

Trust me on this: Writing to you about sex or drugs or integrity—in fact, just about everything else in *Growing Balls*—is a walk in the park compared to writing about unhealthy love relationships. Why? Because it's an almost hopeless task to try and reason with a young guy on a "love high." If you're in love, that's what you're on—the love drug. No matter how clear it might be to his friends (or family) that his relationship is unhealthy, a guy on a love high is blind to the red flags so obvious to everyone else and deaf to whatever they have to say that isn't positive and supportive. When you're on this high, you're sure no one else "gets it." To make things worse, the high you're on feels the same whether or not the relationship is healthy. That's a big problem.

Now I, of course, don't know you or your situation at all. You might be an unusually mature twenty-year-old guy who has happily hooked up with a very early blooming Worthwhile Woman of the same age. Maybe you both *are* ready for a committed relationship; maybe even marriage and children. In this case, almost nothing in this chapter will relate to you—although I would still wonder and ask you, "What exactly is the rush to settle down?" But we'll address that concern later. A very few young people fit into this rare category of relationship readiness since youth and immaturity go hand in hand—and rightly so. Remember the *Growing Balls* take on the immaturity issue: Immaturity is *not* some shameful condition to be overcome. Immaturity is just a stage of development on the way to maturity.

Frankly, I wish it wasn't necessary to question your relationship, but if you're a young man, it is, especially if people who *know* you are worried about you. They may be trying to get through to you about your relationship and you're not listening to them. Worse yet, they may be afraid to say anything to you, fearing your backlash. So, since I don't know you at all—I'm not part of your family *or* your friend—I'm free to take a shot at the subject and walk you through a few questions and ideas that will help you decide if you're making good choices when it comes to girls/women. It's worth your time because, if you think about it, the stakes are pretty high.

Now, it's important to me that I not come off a cynical asshole in this chapter—a battle my wife warns me, after reading my first few swipes at this subject, I have been losing. But I'm not giving up. If you follow your heart (or dick) into a bad or badly timed relationship, you may never find your way back out. While under the influence of the love drug, you may become an unprepared husband, or much worse, an unprepared father. Lots of guys in every generation take on marriage and/or fatherhood before they are ready, often just to prove to someone else how mature they are; many will then unhappily bungle their way through both jobs for years, only realizing their mistakes as they naturally mature over the ensuing years.

By then, however, it's too late. If you fall into that trap, anything you end up doing will be painful for you and everyone else involved, whether you slog through the muck of an unhappy marriage "for the kids" or break it up (the more common response). Don't your future kids deserve better from their dad?

Young Love

What makes young love unhealthy? First of all, not all of it *is* unhealthy. Young people can and do develop genuine and healthy love for one another. It happens—but not as often as you think. Again, maybe none of this relates to you. Maybe you and your girl are the exception to the young-love relationship rule. But just to be on the safe side, or even for the sake of argument, consider that you *might not* be an exception. In that case, you can think of this chapter as a warning, a word to the wise. Since you and your girl may be peaking on the love drug and your vision is, therefore, dangerously blurry, I'll give you a poetic image to think about: This chapter is a lighthouse, nestled among sharp and unforgiving rocks in a relationship fog which has scuttled and sunk the ships of many a love-struck sailor like yourself. How's that?

Here's a quick, two-sentence test for relationships:

In a healthy relationship, the couple in love is bound together more out of desire for each other than out of need. Unhealthy relationships are just the opposite: they need one another too much.

If your friends or family are trying to get through to you about your relationship—they see something wrong—that's probably what's getting their attention. They have seen it before: What's masquerading as mature love isn't. Instead, it is you and your sweetheart caught up in *the need to feel loved and the "high" of feeling in love.*

Okay, that, and lust. You can't ignore lust. Let's face it. Y'all are horny. That's normal too, but you can't ignore the horny part and expect to make good relationship decisions. Young people are *supposed* to be horny. So, while you are focused on convincing the doubters around you that you're "really in love," don't get insulted when they bring up the horny factor. Sexual urges are powerful at any age, but they're off the charts in a young person—and we adults remember, yes, we do. That's why we get so nervous when it comes to young people and sex. Feeling in love, when combined with sex, is explosive. If you and your girl are "in love" right now, you're both absolutely awash in big doses of hormones and other thrilling, feel-good brain chemicals—and they're as powerful as anything you can buy on the street. You're on a full-blown high though you may not know it, especially if this is your first experience with the love drug. You're floating above the rest of us and it feels *great*. You may think that no one understands you because *no one else has ever felt this way*. But we have. It's hard to imagine, I know, but we really have. It's especially hard to understand when we adults are not supporting you in this new love of yours.

Being in love, feeling loved so intensely, is the *best*, isn't it? You feel completely understood by the one you love and you seem to have so much in common. It feels great; which is why you may be resisting any unsupportive input, even from people who really know you. They say they understand what you're going through but you think they can't, right? So you can ignore their doubts and negative comments. Your girl is *special,* right? Your love is *real.* How could anything that feels *this good* not be real?

I understand why you want to ignore the advice around you. And you're right if you're thinking that these people—the disbelievers—probably are *not* going through the same thing you are right now. Their relationships have probably moved on to other, less exciting levels. Or their relationships don't look so healthy, and you know what? Maybe they're not. They themselves might be in unhappy relationships. Either way, you may wonder: Where do they get the nerve to criticize *your* thrilling relationship? Well, they can, despite (or maybe even *because of)* their own relationship problems. Trust me: They know what you are feeling because they, themselves, have felt that same way before, probably a *few* times. Moreover, they know they might be risking their good relationship with you by speaking up. So, no, they're not "just jealous," even if their own relationships suck. Yes, they may envy the high you're on, but that's not why they're speaking up. They're speaking up because they care about you and are brave enough to risk you getting mad at them for telling you the truth as they see it.

They may try to convince you and your girl to back off a little and get some distance from one another for a while—but this almost never works. Actually, it usually backfires. They want you to have some time to at least clear your head a bit before committing yourself to another person. The problem is you two don't feel anything but good—great, actually. Why would you want to back off? You're not feeling overly needy with one other. That's ridiculous, right? You feel in *love.* As far as you two are concerned, you're spending all that time together because you *want* to, not because you *have* to. You don't see yourselves mainlining that mutual adoration like a couple of love junkies, but others do, especially if you're hearing that "Why don't you two try backing off from each other a little for a while?" advice from friends or family. Unfortunately, young people on a need-based love high tend to make bad decisions, just as people do while drunk or high on other kinds of drugs.

Be careful about dismissing the unwanted advice because if it pisses you off there's probably something to it. You know the old expressions: "Where there's smoke, there's fire"; or "If it looks like a duck, walks like a duck, and quacks like a duck, it's probably a duck." Their feedback may not all be on target, or the person offering it may be a pain in the ass, but you may still benefit from thinking through what they're saying.

People who care about you will try to get through to you—for a while. At some point, however, most will give up. They'll figure you're one of those people who need to learn your lessons the hard way. And maybe you are . . .

And maybe you're not. So, are you ready to listen? What exactly are they giving you such a hard time about? The key word (or idea) to listen for is "need." Unhealthy love is based on need. For that matter, *all* unhealthy relationships (whether to a person, alcohol, or other drugs; an image of yourself; a job or other roles we play in life) are based on *too much need*.

Rule of thumb: If you need something more than you want it, your relationship is unhealthy. This rule is at the heart of addiction.

The reason is simple: If you need something more than you want it, you have to have it just to feel okay. Because of your powerful need, you lose your ability to take care of yourself. You have given up your power to someone or something *outside of you*, and you are now at its/their mercy. This is a very insecure and even dangerous way to feel. It's like having religion without faith.

Here's a hands-on, quick example of "want versus need" common to most young men: Drinking. Wanting a drink is okay. Wanting a drink is part of *using* alcohol. People have always used it for its effects on their mood. When used responsibly (like not in excess and *not* before driving), moderate drinking is usually not a problem.

Needing a drink, however: That *is* a problem. You can easily see the difference in people you know. We all have. These are the people who drink *before* they get to the party or who start drinking heavily as soon as they get there. These are the people who plan their free time and socializing around alcohol and fellow drinkers. They avoid sober social situations in favor of those that will involve drinking. These folks *need* their alcohol even more than they want it. They so associate fun with drinking and boredom with sobriety that not drinking is not an option. They *need* to drink. That's a problem situation on its way to getting worse.

So remember: Want versus Need. In a healthy relationship, you want the other more than you need it. Now, since we're talking about your relationships with girls/women, here, let's stick to a relationship example of want versus need.

Wanting a girlfriend is normal but needing one is not and leads to big problems. I'll admit, we all have *some* need in our relationships, but it's the amount that counts. In a healthy relationship, both partners will trade off feeling needy and being strong for the other person. Now and again, when times get tough and our confidence falters, we all feel vulnerable and needy. That's normal. Being able to feel safe and vulnerable at the same time is one of the benefits of being in a good and committed long-term relationship.

On the other hand, people who pretend to "not need anybody" are unrealistic and probably fooling themselves. Some need is normal in any relationship and the amount will change depending on life circumstances. Keep this in mind, however: the safe zone, in terms of neediness, is pretty limited. Cross the line into being *too* needy *too* often and you'll push your partner or even your friends away, especially if you are not working on your issues to be stronger. People like this exhaust and wear down their friends.

In a relationship, you're expected to work on your issues and problems to avoid weighing down and frustrating your partner. When you get too needy, when it becomes unhealthy, you may not see it right away. But other people, those who know you well, will. I'm sure you have seen this problem in other people. Movies and songs are full of stories of needy people in unhealthy relationships. It's an old pattern you've seen a hundred times. A guy and a girl get together. And in the beginning, it's great. They are attracted to each other and have fun together. Meanwhile, in the flush of early love (high as kites on the love drug), they both ignore little signs and red flags of problems to come. They focus on the fun of loving and feeling loved, of feeling adored.

For our example here, let's say the girl in this new love relationship starts getting a little uncomfortable. She loves her guy, sure, but he acts a little weird sometimes. When he drinks he gets too possessive, like asking too many questions about where she goes and whom she is with when he's not around. At other times, let's say he tries too hard for her attention, that sort of thing. It's not bad at first, nothing too serious, and she lets it go. After all, he has great qualities too.

From his perspective, all is normal. He just knows that he loves her and as long as he has her, life is good. But it isn't healthy love. He wants her, sure, but he needs her much more. He *needs* to have a girlfriend; otherwise, he doesn't feel good about himself. Since this problem is not immediately apparent to his girl, things are fine for a while. However, when she wants some elbow room to be with her friends or to spend some time alone, his "neediness" problem comes out.

At this point, her friends usually start making negative comments to her about him behind his back. They warn her to "watch out for that guy." And no matter what she says to defend him, deep down, she knows they're on to something. She may deny the problem in the beginning, but eventually, she starts listening and begins pulling back a little from the relationship.

This is when Mr. Needy starts to panic, but he tries to stay cool. He tries getting the relationship back under control by pushing her to spend even more time together. He'll start spending more money on her or doing her too many special favors. He's trying too hard. If she starts pulling away, he may think she's seeing someone else, which, even if it isn't true, soon will be because he's starting to act creepy. Neediness is making an insecure, but otherwise good guy, act creepy.

This is a very typical scenario. Usually, it's a pretty harmless situation. The couple argues. They make up. They argue more. They break up. This cycle may repeat a few times before the breakup takes for good.

A small but dangerous group of guys in this position get aggressive. When they get nervous, they try controlling their girl's every move and telling her whom she can and can't hang out with. If the girl is not strong emotionally or the guy is scary, she'll obey for a while until her friends convince her to cut bait and dump him.

Other guys also come on strong, but in a wimpy way. They call the girl too much and complain if she's not available. They'll ask things like, "I called you last night and you weren't home. Where were you? Who were you with?" This act turns creepy fast, and again, the girl's friends (the only people she is likely to listen to) will convince her to dump him and run. Either way, needy guys end up putting pressure on their girlfriends for more attention, which only pushes them away.

The bottom line is this: Neediness is a weakness, and, brother, it isn't attractive. In fact, women are most attracted to guys who come across as not seeming to need them at all (the Bad Boy's successful tactic, remember?). That comes across as confidence. A Worthwhile Woman knows that she and her man will both feel needy sometimes and that's normal. But she doesn't want to feel like she's her man's mommy. And that's alarmingly common. You'd be surprised how many grown women often think of their husbands as just another one of their kids. I hear that a lot and it's sickening.

Needy guys may try to buy their girl's affection and loyalty with presents and expensive dates—which may work for a while. But soon enough, most women see this pathetic behavior for what it is and move on anyway. If a girl/woman has any integrity, she'll break up with the guy rather than string him along for the free goodies. If not, she'll take him for all he's worth, lie to him, cheat on him, and then, finally, dump him.

The sad thing is, a few of these needy guys end up killing themselves—the ultimate proof that, without a girlfriend to make them feel whole, they have no sense of self. Fortunately, that's rare. More often, here's what happens: The girl coming out of a relationship with a needy guy sees him slink away for good after he leaves some pitiful "come back to me" notes, emails, or phone messages as icing on his too-needy cake. There are plenty of "I can't live without you" songs to serve as the soundtrack for this scenario.

Then there's the other extreme, where things don't go so smoothly. If she's *not* so lucky, the boyfriend or husband she has left, now feeling fully exposed for the needy guy he is, becomes *dangerous*. Maybe he ends up stalking her, scaring her, and generally trying to make her life miserable. And remember, this is the guy who claims to *love* her. Where is the love in that kind of behavior?

What's the worst-case scenario? Needy Guy morphs into a "If *I* can't have you then *no one will*" kind of guy. You can read about these guys in your newspaper just about every week—I did just this morning. In this case, a guy's wife was divorcing him; the paper didn't go into why she left him but it did say they were married as teenagers—what a surprise, eh? Unable to handle her rejection and apparently having no self-esteem without her, this guy went to her house in the middle of the night and killed her. But first, and right in front of her, he killed three of their kids. Then, and not surprisingly, he killed himself, proving that he couldn't live without her. There's that soundtrack again: All those soupy "love songs" with guys singing "I can't live without you" don't sound so sweet or romantic now, do they?

Unfortunately, no matter how mature or tough this boy/man looked or acted when this tragic couple got together, he got married and became a father before growing any balls. When times got tough, he looked inside himself and found nothing—no tools to help him handle his growing feelings of impotent rage. He was just like an angry little boy on the playground who punches other kids when he gets his feelings hurt. As much as I hate his actions and mourn their consequences, I have empathy for that boy who, though his body matured into that of a mature man, never actually became one.

That is an example of a pretty sick guy, I know, and *Growing Balls* is not a book guys like him will read—so I don't imagine you, who is reading this, to be much like him. Nor do I imagine *Growing Balls* helping this guy much if he had read it. A guy who kills people who hurt his feelings has been a mess for a long time. The breakup just put him over the edge. The sad thing, however, is he started out just like you and me, right? A baby boy full of promise and hope for a good life.

Most boys and men who have had—and overcome—the "neediness problem" are *way* healthier, from the start, than our sick brother from the newspaper and nowhere near as dangerous. But until we grew some balls, we were often miserable in our relationships. Rough times in a relationship are normal, but day-to-day unhappiness and frustration is no way to live. We didn't actually get violent, but we may have fantasized violence. We might have said and done stupid, mean things to get our paybacks. No one likes feeling weak or insecure.

What kind of stupid and mean things? Check out some signs of neediness for more normal, nonviolent (nice) guys. Ask yourself if you've thought or acted like this in your relationship.

1. You feel angry at things she does or says, but instead of confronting her, you act cool, like it doesn't bother you. *Don't fool yourself into believing you're easygoing and she's not. You just don't have the balls to tell her how you really feel. You're selling yourself out. Worse yet, after a while you'll end up doing or saying stupid stuff to even the score. See number five below.*

2. Instead of planning a date, you usually ask her what *she* wants to do. *Women hate this. You are either trying too hard to please her (which makes you look weak) or you're just lazy. Neither is attractive.*

3. You put women on a pedestal. *This is a huge mistake. Women don't like being worshipped. For one thing, they know they don't deserve it; for another, it makes you look weak. They know their weaknesses and don't respect you for being blind to them. Remember, people put others on a pedestal before knocking them down, and that's exactly what you'll eventually do. The more you idealize a woman, the bitchier she'll get. If your girlfriend or wife acts like a bitch most of the time, it's probably your fault. She's waiting for you to grow some balls and demand to be treated with some respect. There is a big difference between treating a woman well (with affection and respect) and putting her on a pedestal and worshipping her. Figure it out. You absolutely have to figure this out.*

4. You feel jealous of other people who get her time and attention, like her friends, her family—even her pets—and try to guilt her into giving you more of her time. *If you want more of a woman's time, just ask for it. If you don't get it, you're simply not that high on her priority list—at least, not right now. (Sorry.) If you stop and think about it, you may find you have slipped into that weak position of needing her even more than you want her, and you know what that means. Or you and the girl/woman*

may just not be on the same page when it comes to the relationship. Either way, you now have three choices: (1) Decide you can be happy (or at least okay, for now) with things as they are; (2) Work out a compromise with her to get more of what you want and need from the relationship; (3) Move on and find someone who is a better fit for you. Those are the only three choices for a man with balls. However, no matter what, don't whine to her—you may as well wear an "I'm Needy "sign on your forehead.

5. You purposefully do things that drive her nuts. There is an endless list of possibilities here and all couples are different. But comedians make their living talking about this stuff. They bust men for "forgetting" things that are important to her. Need some examples? How about not calling when we said we would? Showing up late or not at all for agreed upon plans? Getting loaded in situations when she has asked us to stay sober or drink reasonably? Or for couples who live together, leaving messes in the kitchen or dirty clothes and wet towels on the floor; "forgetting" to write down messages from her friends or her mother; forgetting anniversaries, birthdays, and so on. *In the therapy business, we call this passive-aggressive behavior. If you're doing any of this, you're not being honest about your own frustrations and other feelings so you get your paybacks in nasty little ways, while pretending not to. It's very weak, especially if you then whine about how picky or bitchy she is, or complain about how she doesn't appreciate the other things you do.*

The needy problem occurs with women, too, of course. The difference with needy girls (at the crazy level) is, when *they* get desperate, their violence tends to be self-inflicted. Sometimes, they'll act out and tear up your stuff, like messing with your car or wrecking something else important to you. Fortunately for guys, though crazy women sometimes try to kill the guys who dump them, they are much more likely to hurt or kill themselves instead. But don't worry too much about that. Because before they get suicidal, most needy girls like this first try to hook the guy in by getting pregnant. Does that make you feel better? No?

When a needy guy feels his girl pulling away, he tries buying her back. It's kind of pitiful, sure, but pretty harmless. But when a girl like this feels her guy pulling away, she reels him back in with sex—sometimes, minus the birth control. And we guys aren't all that hard to catch, are we? When the "little head" jumps in and takes charge, we may hang in there with a girl we plan to dump—just long enough to make an unwanted baby.

So, what do all these horror stories have to do with you and your relationship? You don't see yourself or your girl in *any* of this? Wonderful. That's excellent. Those stories are all about crazy people, right? Your young love may be the healthy exception. I'm open to that idea. However, before you decide that's the case, listen to what the people who *know you well* are saying about your relationship. If they're not saying anything, ask them. Tell them you want to hear the truth. They may very well have opinions they've been afraid to share with you. Are they supportive or worried? Let's look at what you might hear, from best to worst.

Scenario number one: They (and I mean more than one or two people your age) are supportive of your relationship. They give you the "thumbs-up" and encourage you to go full steam ahead. *Okay, you probably don't need any advice this chapter has to offer.*

Scenario number two: They think you are too busy getting laid to notice you have a very needy girl on your hands. *You're in deep shit. Only you can avoid the huge mess coming your way. Re-read this chapter and the rest of the book carefully.*

Scenario number three: Your trusted advisors told you they think *you* are the needy one. *Okay, this is not good. But as painful messages go, it's a double-edged sword. Thank your lucky stars that at least someone is being honest with you. And props to you for asking for the truth. That said, however, you are in much deeper shit than the guy from scenario number two. You have to get on a treatment plan, my friend, and quick, before it's too late and you do something stupid or dangerous that you'll have to live with forever. Here's what to do:*

a. *Start spending more time with your male friends.*

b. *Give up dating for a while until you feel stronger.*

c. *Find an older, more experienced guy to talk to—your dad, an uncle or a family friend you can trust—and get honest. Don't feel bad: You're not the first guy to feel insecure about yourself and women. Most important, start preparing for how you're going to handle the end of the relationship, because most likely, the light you see at the end of the tunnel is really the breakup train heading your way.*

d. *If there is not such a man in your life, try going to a male therapist. This may sound like a radical suggestion but it really isn't. You go to a dentist when you have a toothache, don't you? Maybe not right away, but when the pain in your tooth doesn't respond to extra brushing and flossing, you bite the bullet and go to the dentist and get the problem fixed by a professional. Think of the money you spend going to a therapist as an investment in your future. I promise it will be far cheaper than a divorce or criminal lawyer.*

e. *If you have older sisters or aunts, quietly seek their advice too. They can be quite helpful because they know your story. They know your parents and understand how you got to be the way you are. Basically, they more or less understand what makes you, you. Plus, they've watched you with girls/ women all your life and can give you the brutal truth, if you have the balls to listen to it. Your mom might be willing to listen and offer advice too, but she is, after all, your mom and maybe a little too biased in your favor to be of much real help. She'll probably tell you that your girl wasn't good enough for you,*

f. *Find a hobby you like and start spending time developing your skills. Get really good at something, or even a few things. Nothing builds a guy's self-esteem like having a couple areas of expertise. We all need to feel proud of ourselves. Give yourself reasons to feel proud. Exercise your body and your mind. When times are tough and you feel low, you need to look inside and see something there of substance.*

g. *Most important of all:* **Don't ever again rely on a woman to make you feel good about yourself.**

Scenario number four: People who know you well are saying that your girl *is* terrific, but they feel that you two are just too young to be so deeply involved. *Now, this is a tough one because hearing it is hard on the ego. The clear message is "You're too immature to be this serious with someone." Consider the following:*

We're back to discussing the variations on the word "mature." Remember, in the wider American culture, it is embarrassing to be considered immature. Remember that immaturity refers to the state of not yet being ready. That's all. We don't expect a young, newly formed sports team to compete evenly with an established and experienced one. Now and then a young team pulls off a miracle, but most often, experience and maturity win out as expected. No one *blames* the young team for being immature. Players need to learn one another's thoughts and moves. This takes time. Loyal fans have to be patient and look forward to the team's potential being realized through practice, experience, and good coaching.

This all makes sense. But somehow, a young man not being ready for a relationship—being immature—this is a cause for shame. How ridiculous. And yet, this is a common way of thinking. So don't be surprised that you respond defensively when someone you trust "accuses" you of being too young or immature. The accusation may sting a little and embarrass you. Don't let it. Remember, you are *not* being told you've hooked up with a nutcase. The feedback on your girl (and your judgment) is fine; you're just too young to commit yourself to anyone.

If this is the case, from my position, I say, congratulations! You apparently know how to spot a good/worthwhile girl/woman and how to develop a healthy relationship with her. Take a bow, dude. It's a rare skill among boys and young men. This also means *you have grown some balls already*. Excellent. Now, instead of taking the next step towards commitment, you're free to focus your young energies in other needed areas of personal growth. Maybe this relationship will last; maybe it won't. It depends on whether or not the girl/woman can wait for you to be ready for a commitment to the relationship and to her. Unfortunately, *you have no control over this*.

Meanwhile, at your age, ask yourself this question: What exactly is the rush to be committed for life to one person? Why do you have to stop meeting new girls just because you found one good one? There are other good ones out there too. You don't have to stop seeing this person—*unless she expects a commitment from you*. This means essentially pretending you're engaged. Is that what you want? Would that make you feel like a man? Are you *afraid* to have a less committed relationship? If so, why? Are you worried she will meet someone else and leave you? If that is your fear then you better face up to it now because *you are the needy guy we've been talking about*. Sure, you're not the violent nutcase, but you're *way too needy* if you're committing yourself to a relationship before you're ready *out of fear of losing the girl*. And believe me; tons of guys have done this. Sometimes it works out; often it does not.

Meanwhile, if you *decline* the commitment she just might go off and find someone else. Remember, if *she* feels ready for a commitment, she probably will and probably should. Why should she put her life on hold for you? There are other good and worthwhile guys out there for her too. Hopefully, she'll hook up with a guy who *is* ready. However, just as likely, she'll find a guy no more prepared for a relationship than you are, especially if I'm right that a woman seeks out men who are ready for about the same amount of intimacy as she herself can handle.

If this happens, what exactly would that say about your special love? Was it really *you* she wanted or does she really just want (need?) a boyfriend or a husband (and a baby)? These are painful questions to think about, I know, but it is better to face up to them now than to have the nagging worry that they're true. Keep this in mind: Fear of losing someone is *not* a good foundation for a lasting relationship; in fact, it is one of the *worst* reasons to stay together. Also, relationships that are too serious, too soon, are rarely going to be healthy.

My advice? If you don't feel ready for a commitment and your girl is still pressuring you for one, even if she seems like a good and Worthwhile Woman, break up and move on. You can always get back together later, if that's the right thing to do.

Unfortunately, whether you're in a healthy relationship or not, the great feeling you get from "being in love" is the same. But just because it *feels* right doesn't mean it *is* right. This is hard for a young person to grasp, but it's true. We older guys have lived through a few rounds of this and now know better— but no one wants to believe us.

My friends and I have discovered an interesting thing: Our feelings are real but they may not reflect reality. For instance, let's say you are a rich guy and a young woman decides to go after you for access to your money. She can *pretend* to love you, and if you don't notice any dishonesty (or ignore the red flags others may see), *it will feel real* to you. Until you find out you are being used, her "love," if she's a good actress, will feel like the real thing. That's why betrayal hurts so damn much. Even if your feelings for her are real, the relationship itself cannot be. This is why people with some relationship experience are so gun-shy about love. They *know* how good it is going to feel if they let themselves "fall in love." They want to relax and enjoy the great feelings you are feeling now. But from experience, they also know how much it is going to hurt if they end up getting burned. So they're smart and take it slow. The rush of the love drug may not be as intense when taken in measured doses as compared to "falling in love," but it is easier to relax and enjoy the good feelings.

In your life, you will know (and read about) many people who, time after time, "fall in love" recklessly, plunging headfirst into passionate relationships that inevitably crash and burn. These people are hooked on the *rush* of a massive dose of the love drug so that, despite painful breakups, they do the same thing, the same way, over and over again. The "right one" is always the *next* one. Never mind that any one of the ruined relationships *might* have grown into a healthy one had they tried working on improving themselves first. Their downfall is the need for the fireworks and passion of a movie-style "love at first sight." Most of these people end up, after many miserable relationships, old, bitter, and alone. I don't want you to end up like this, nor do the people in your life who care about you.

Meanwhile, I have empathy for these people too, because I do remember what the big dose of the love drug feels like. It is powerful and so are my memories of it. The high beats any chemical drug I ever tried. New love is more delicious than any food and only moments of pure creativity or spirituality are more powerful. So, I know what I'm up against here.

So, you're in love? Here's the Brutal Truth: There is more than one person out there for you to love and to love you back.

The popular notion that in this life there is only one person in the world for you to love and to love you in return, is a *myth*. It is romantic nonsense. Don't fall for it. People under the influence of new (or lost) love often believe it because their feelings for this person are so powerful that it **must** be true. But it isn't. There are no shortages of Worthwhile Women for Men with Balls. But if you fall for that "one love in this life" line of crap, you're going to be desperate when your "one true love" is gone.

New (immature) love may, over time and effort, mature into the real deal—but usually it doesn't (sorry). That blast of ecstasy you feel with new love is a delicious illusion. It is certainly a *possibility* of love, and that's nothing to sneeze at. That's wonderful. If with time and shared experiences it does evolve into real love, great; but, brother, it ain't love at the beginning. Real love, like real friendship, takes time to develop and cure. It is developed and strengthened by sharing the good times and surviving the hard ones; by feeling soulful connections and working through painful misunderstandings. Love evolves while working through hurt feelings and nursing one another through grief and fear. The long-term payoff is slow but sweet.

Love is earned. So, take it slow. When you are ready (mature enough) for a love relationship, enjoy the rush of the love drug since it doesn't last forever. You don't want to be a tight-ass, so sure, let yourself go a little nuts, but hold off signing any papers or making any verbal commitments until you know what you are getting yourself into. Since we tend to take too big a bite of the love-drug when it comes our way, give yourself time to level out before making any big decisions. Let the dust settle a little and gain some needed perspective. Listen to the people who know you well. They won't all be right, but at least hear them out. If you're afraid to listen or can't bear to hear their criticism, then dollars to donuts, they probably *are* right.

If you can, remind yourself of the Brutal Truth: there are *many* people in the world to love and to love you in return. Doing so will give you more options when it comes time to make an important decision. If you allow it, you will have these same loving feelings with, and for, other people in the future—maybe several people. I know this is hard to believe. But look at the divorce rate (about 50 percent) and consider that all these people felt just like you do now when *they* got married.

*   *   *

How then do you improve your chances of a happy, long-lasting marriage? For starters, get some clarity on love—which is not easy to do. Love is hard to define, and the feelings that go with it are so powerful that they often transcend words, which is why so many songs are written with love as their theme. It is easier, then, to say what love is *not*:

1. Love is not selfish or possessive.

Listen to all the needy bullshit in those love songs we happily hum along to on the radio, and keep this in mind: The relationships in those songs are *almost always* unhealthy. The "I can't live without you" sentiments and protests of "you're the only girl for me" are sick. I'm a sucker for a good tune too, believe me, but *do we want our kids listening to this sort of crap?* I'm only half kidding here. I'm not for censoring music but honestly; don't expect to learn about healthy relationships from the radio. What sells records (oops . . . , I mean CDs) is a catchy tune and lyrics people can relate to, and people relate to feeling "in love" or broken in two with pain over a breakup. Songs that scratch these itches have lyrics that just *drip* with neediness. What normal woman wants a guy to need her that much? What if she changes her mind about him? Does she want a guy who's ready to kill himself if she meets someone she likes better? Do you want a girl to need *you* that much?

The "want versus need" thing bears repeating here: If you **need** the relationship even more than you **want** it, it is unhealthy. This litmus test works for any kind of relationship. Think about it. When you are too needy, you have no power to take care of yourself. You are at the mercy of another—and how can that be good?

2. Love is not temporary.

Real love lives on, even though we "fall out of love." That's why our old relationships still mean something to us and are sometimes a source of jealousy to new and insecure girlfriends and wives. I, for one, will always love my old girlfriends.

3. Love is not instant.

There is no such thing as "love at first sight." Love, however, may *spark* suddenly. The "spark suddenly" experience—which *is* real—is the "love at first sight" we hear about or have experienced. It's not the real thing yet, but it has that *potential.* Something is telling you, in that instant, "This could really be something" and it just might be true. That experience, unsettling to married people or those who believe in the "one person on earth for me to love" theory, is just more evidence that, in fact, there *are* many potential partners for us in the world, even if we choose to stay with only one.

4. New love is not realistic, which is okay as long as you realize it.

The eyes of new lovers become rose-colored mirrors where, in the beginning, they see only the best in each other. This is a symptom of the love-drug high, which is why it cannot be completely trusted even while it is being enjoyed. The same quirky stuff about your girlfriend that you laugh off now (or ignore) will be a pain in the ass once you have been married for a while. Any married couple will tell you this, even those happily married. They had to work out an arrangement on those issues to be happy. This rose-colored-mirror phenomenon makes new love completely unrealistic. In reality, people are many sided and complicated. But the love-drug is so powerful that someone riding the high of strong dose may not even realize his feelings are unrealistic, or he may indeed know the truth and still not care. It's that good.

5. New love, therefore, especially for young people is not really about love; it is about adoring and being adored.

New love for inexperienced lovers is all about adoring, and being adored by, your beloved. For most of us, the "falling in love" experience is the first time anybody besides our parents focused such adoration upon us. And how great is that? You feel on top of the world because another person thinks *you* are the greatest person on it. In grateful recognition, you return the feeling. Suddenly, you both can ditch your fears and insecurities and focus on making this suddenly very important person, happy. If they're happy, you'll be happy. Locked in this happy bondage, the two of you are now—for a while—glued at the hip.

And the sex? The *sex*? What can I say? It is beyond description, right? The *amazing sex* is proof enough to new lovers that anything anyone says about their new relationship that isn't *totally supportive* is complete bullshit: ignorant, jealous bullshit.

Except it isn't.

Like any other delicious drug, new love begs for moderation and perspective. When you're young and inexperienced in the "ways of love," it is very easy to put your eggs in one basket and find yourself hopelessly dependent on another person.

Trust me: This is a mistake.

CHAPTER NINE

"Yes, Dear" My Ass

The Myth of the Henpecked Husband

Right from the start, when it comes to getting our own needs met, we boys are given warning that our relationships with our girlfriends, and eventually our wives, are going to suck (and not in the ways we hope). Again, it starts with the damn cartoons. Guys my age remember old cartoons from the fifties that showed small timid husbands and their huge angry and overwhelming wives blasting them with demands and complaints. In response, the husband typically repeated his ball-less mantra, ("yes, dear . . . yes, dear") while cowering in fear and rushing to do whatever she told him to do. He never confronted her and *never* said no; if he tried, she'd have crushed him like a bug. If he got back at her at all, it was by going behind her back and being sneaky—that passive-aggressive behavior we looked at in the last chapter.

The modern and most famous cartoon dad, *Homer Simpson*, has some of this going on with his wife, *Marge*, but as my twelve-year-old son, Noah, remarked, "She embraces his stupidity." There is still some "yes, dear" stuff going on there, but Homer and Marge are a step up for the typical relationship dynamic of weak husband/nagging-wife, so maybe things are looking up a little. Noah, however, assures me that there are still plenty of weak "yes, dear" cartoon guys on television. When I ask him and his friends about this, they all say they know what I am talking about and they've never even watched the *Flintstones* or the *Jetsons*.

But it's not just in cartoons that we boys are warned about what is to come once we commit ourselves to a girl. Movies, television shows, and commercials love to show the man/father acting like a bumbling fool, struggling to figure out how to have some fun on the sly. We see guys jumping through all sorts of hoops as they try to figure out how to make and keep their girlfriends or wives happy. Women are treated like some sort of prize the guy doesn't really deserve. He's supposed to feel lucky for any positive attention he gets.

It's pathetic. Most often, the harder the guy tries, the more miserably he fails. While he looks foolish and undignified, consider the messages getting communicated to the boys and young men watching him. They are seeing relationships in a very negative light, and this notion is repeated in popular culture generation after generation. And women wonder why we guys aren't in any hurry to commit to them? Where are the examples of Men with Balls in healthy relationships with Worthwhile Women? You have to look hard for examples of healthy relationships in popular culture.

Do you need a non-media example of the man's weak position in society? Take a look at what couples traditionally do on the eve of getting married. The following description of the pre-wedding ritual is not true of everyone, of course, but it is certainly common. See if you recognize some of this from you own observations of our culture.

First of all, on the night before our wedding, we men are encouraged to have a bachelor party where the explicit message is "This is your last night of fun." Our best friend, the best man, is supposed to put this party together for us. Even if the groom doesn't actually have sex "one last time" with a stranger brought to the party for that very reason, he still is supposed to get very drunk and have some sort of female sexual attention from a woman *other* than his fiancée. On the tame side, he gets lap dances at a strip bar or his friends hire a stripper to dance for the evening. On the wilder side, his buddies may actually set him up to have sex. If a guy is doing this on the night before he gets married, do you really think he's ready and willing to make that life-long commitment? Why is he risking his marriage on the night before it starts? Seems strange, doesn't it? But this is a well-worn tradition. Why is that?

Meanwhile, his blushing bride-to-be isn't supposed to protest the bachelor party (though some do). Instead, she is supposed to pretend not to think about what he is doing at his bachelor party (assuming he won't go "too far"). She is supposed to let him "get it out of his system." Her girlfriends, meanwhile, get her drunk enough not to care about what he may be doing on his last night of freedom. At these bachelorette parties, many a bride-to-be has been known to get into some action of her own on *her* last night of freedom with her stripper or boy-toy, but that is rarely discussed.

Meanwhile, back at the bachelor party, the groom's single friends are warning him—as they get him drunk off his ass—that once he's married he won't be having much fun with them anymore. No matter how he denies it, his married friends, for the most part, sadly support the notion. The bachelor protests that his fiancée "is cool—she won't mind me going out." His friends look at each other, shake their heads and say, "Sure, man, sure. We'll see." Then they pour the naïve bastard another drink.

They know that if his wife is in the least bit typical, he can forget the idea of spare time, because she already has a long list of things she wants them to do *together*, plus an endless list of chores and projects she expects him to do. Again, this is the typical story. It's not true of everybody. Let's hope our guy is marrying a Worthwhile Woman. She will *support* his need to maintain his friendships just as she will expect him to support her need to maintain hers. A Man with Balls and a Worthwhile Woman make a couple that respects individual needs and desires. They balance their "together activities" with separate ones. This has the added benefit of giving them more to talk about when they are together.

For the sake of example, however, let's say our guy has *some balls,* his friends see him as a stand-up guy, but in his relationships with women, he's never quite learned to establish and hold on to his power. Because of this, he's been caught in a ball-shrinking, power-sapping vortex ever since he decided to "pop the question." And while we are on the subject of proposing marriage, let's look at the silly setup society handed him from the start. If our boy already had a hard time holding on to his power in the relationship, his proposal ritual didn't help his cause any. Check it out and forgive me the stereotyping along the way. This stuff is way too common to ignore.

According to tradition, a man is supposed to propose to his bride-to-be *while down on one knee*—to my eyes, begging, like a dog, for her "hand" in marriage. Oh yeah, this is a *great start* for a balanced relationship. Both people will surely be equal partners when one starts out *literally below the other.* The typical fiancée will be expecting this "one-down" routine. Only she won't see it the way I am describing it. She'll see it as the most romantic moment of her life, the one she has dreamed of since she was a little girl, playing prince-and-princess games with her dolls. It is as programmed into her to be begged for by her husband-to-be as it is programmed into him to do the begging. I don't blame her for expecting it and I don't blame him for doing it. Still, that doesn't make it a good idea or a healthy start for a marriage. And there's more.

According to tradition, when a man proposes marriage, he should hold in his hand a diamond engagement ring—essentially a bribe to his intended for agreeing to and promising to marry him—which is expected to cost the equivalent of *three months* of his work pay. If a guy spends anything less, he is considered cheap. The size of the rock is a symbol of his worth as a husband, like a big diamond makes him a "good catch" (another weird image, don't you think?). A less expensive ring is also seen as a slight on the wife-to-be. She sees the size of the rock on her finger as a sign of how he sees *her* worth too.

So, what's the story here? Is this guy marrying a wife or putting down a deposit on a lifetime hooker? (Maybe that sounds harsh, but many a real hooker has pointed out that her job contract with her john isn't much different compared with that of a husband to a wife, except for the time involved. It's more up front and direct about expectations of the relationship too.) Sure, some engagements begin with a more modest and reasonable ring purchase and the woman is perfectly happy. This makes *her* a good catch, and more power to the couple for putting love over image—but doing so means bucking tradition. Even in these cases where either: (1) good sense triumphs over tradition; or (2) limited available money forces the more reasonable choice of a modest ring, the social expectation is still there for the big rock. Deep down, the guy may always *wish he could have bought* the big ring, just as she may always secretly wish she had gotten one. When he "makes it" someday (financially), he'll likely buy his wife the splashy ring and tell her she really deserved it from the start.

Again, is this true of everyone? Of course not. But we are all exposed to these popular notions of value and self-worth and ignoring or overcoming them takes some work. The average kids growing up today are exposed to these same expectations through popular culture and especially through advertising. If no one helps them see that they have more choices than the traditional ones, they're likely to fall into the old traps.

Think of a young guy spending three months' salary on a ring! This kind of nonsense drives me nuts! Unless he has a wad of money in the bank, our love-struck guy is going to start his relationship by going into debt. One of the most stressful issues for married couples is money and how it is handled. I guess it is just practice for the future for a young man to put himself into stressful debt before the marriage even gets off the ground. The next thing he knows if he isn't careful, he'll be locked into an endless spending cycle, buying things he doesn't care about or can't really afford in a hopeless effort to keep his wife and kids happy.

By the way, keep in mind I'm talking about *you* here. I'm using an example of "some guy," but you better read this as meaning *you* because this is normal, everyday stuff. This is what you've been taught to expect of marriage. Now, Worthwhile Women have more sense than to be ruled by these traditions and have the good sense to pass them by. Such women want Men with Balls; they wouldn't expect or even want their man on one knee begging for them. Still, this weekend there will be weddings all over the country that started with proposals just the way I described them.

What's all this about? Why do so many men give up their power when they enter a relationship? What are the *unwritten rules of the contract* that we unknowingly sign when we hook up with a woman? If you're married now, you *know* there is an *unwritten contract* between you two, filled with rules on all those subjects you didn't talk about before you got married. There are big and small topics in this contract. And because nothing is written down, it's nearly impossible for both people to be on the same page.

What are the big three topics?

1. money management
2. sex
3. free time

And these are just the big ones. As is said about contracts, the devil is in the details. Start dealing with the day-to-day details of living, from household chores to shopping, cooking, working, and paying bills and you see how important it is to get clear with each other on who is expecting what from whom. And this is all just about the marriage contract. When you add kids to the mix, the picture gets *much* more complicated. Parenting styles within couples differ wildly, which leads to all sorts of general family craziness if they are not worked out to both people's satisfaction.

Much of this can be worked out pretty well if you and your beloved talk about these things before you get married. But usually people do not. For one thing, these are not romantic discussions. If you do talk about them, you may find out how incompatible you are with your intended spouse. People instinctively know that this kind of talk can be a cold shower on a good love high. Most people in love don't want to risk this. They would rather stay ignorant and hope for the best, assuming that "everything will work out *because we love each other.*"

If only that were true. When it comes to an area of disagreement, one partner usually believes he or she will change the other's mind. And there can be some truth to that. In couples that make it, they have developed the skill of successful compromise. Obviously, for the less successful couples, the opposite is true.

This ability to negotiate compromises is vital to a successful marriage. "Yes, dear" rarely works in the long run. And if a couple doesn't come to agreements on the big three topics (money management, free-time management, and sex), once they become parents, their frustrations on those things get thrown into the parenting pot. The kids become excuses for why and how money management, time management, and sex decisions are made.

This is tricky because the arrival of kids does complicate these issues. They and the many other smaller issues couples face in marriage have to be renegotiated regularly. But I'm not talking about renegotiating expectations and agreements as life situations change. I am talking about what happens *when couples don't negotiate their differences* but instead stumble from circumstance to circumstance, hoping it will all work out. When this happens, husbands and wives start "getting back" at one another by turning their kids into sticks they use to whack at one another. For example, they may undermine one another's authority. Dad may enforce only the rules he agrees with, making him the fun parent and Mom the mean one. Or Mom holds off on consequences for breaking the rules, making Dad the punishing parent ("Wait 'til you father gets home . . .") so he gets stuck being the bad guy.

Most of this nonsense could be avoided if couples were willing to have some real conversations about the kind of life they want to have together. Of course, kids *do* change a couple's priorities, but this doesn't have to mean no sex after parenthood or no money for adult play or no time for adult friends. That happens when kids are used as an excuse for not meeting your partner's needs. If a couple can avoid that pitfall, they can negotiate those changes in priorities as challenges arise. It's not that hard, but it's rare.

Why do couples so often avoid these conversations?

1. We're afraid of the big fight (and even breakup) that might result.
2. We're afraid of the accountability. If we get clear about expectations, there will be no more gray area, no more wiggle room. As long as the rules are unclear, we can't be accused of breaking them.

3. We trick ourselves into thinking we "have an understanding" with our partners on these issues. Again, no clarity means no accountability. We avoid asking the questions on the heavy subjects when we don't really want to hear the answers.

Heavy topics are the last subjects couples want to face up to before getting married. Money, sex, free time, chores, and parenting styles: These are the fodder of divorce, my young friend, and engaged couples instinctively know that. It's part of why half of those marriages don't make it.

Know and say out loud what is okay with you and what is not before you sign on the dotted line. You can and should compromise on some things, but you need to know what they are or you'll find yourself defending (or backing down on) all your decisions.

While you're dating, you can pretend all you want that everything will be great when you and your hottie get married. But if you two are heading toward the next level of commitment and still leave those subjects untouched, you're just lighting a slow burning fuse leading nowhere good. Everyone brings assumptions and expectations into a marriage. They come from fantasies of what a good wife or husband is supposed to be. Trust me on this. Sit with the average couple in marriage counseling (which means the relationship has already gone pretty sour) and you'll hear (like I have) men and women complain that their spouses "aren't doing what they're supposed to do." Get them to explain out loud exactly what they believe a husband or wife "is supposed to do" and watch their partner's jaw drop. "You never told me you expected me to blah, blah, blah this, that, or the other thing." And they're right. It *was* never said out loud, it was just assumed and expected. Sometimes couples break up during or as a result of counseling because it becomes clear that their expectations are never going to match up.

This pattern is so distressingly common that a guy with balls *has to take an early stand in his relationships* and make the unclear clear. Otherwise, he gets in line with the other miserable saps who come to expect not to get their needs met without being sneaky. If half of marriages fail, do you really think that the rest of them are happy ones? What do you suppose is the percentage of *happily married couples*? Twenty percent? Thirty? Do most married people look happy to you? Are (or were) *your parents* happy together? Happy marriages don't just happen. People in happy marriages are brave folks who put time in to work on their marriages. They have the tough conversations. They renegotiate their rules now and again.

Couples in new love don't want to lose that magical love-drug feeling, so they fall back on the assumption everything will be okay *because* they are in love. They hope for the best, believing in love's ability to conquer all. But that's a fairytale notion, a false belief. Love doesn't conquer all. In fact, when their love fades and finally fails, society—the rest of us—are left to deal with the consequences of such poorly planned relationships: a staggering divorce rate and countless kids being raised in miserable or broken homes by angry, frustrated, and exhausted single parents.

Finally, then, any couple that marries without first seeing a marriage counselor (or experienced clergyman) to look at these issues is playing Russian roulette with their future. If your relationship can't handle the process of looking at the issues which regularly sink marriages, the magic you two feel is not magic at all: it is just an illusion. Play the "We're special, he's not talking about us" game if you want. But first, talk to other married men about all this if you think I'm wrong. I'm pretty confident of what you will hear.

*   *   *

Now, before we risk whining about men being the victims of society's silly expectations, let's get a hold of ourselves and recognize a couple of things. For one thing, men have choices. We do not have to cave in to society's expectations. We can be strong and do what we believe to be best for us. We are free to compromise as we wish. We can choose to buy our fiancées the big rock. What we can't compromise on is honesty. We have to be honest with our mates and ourselves. There are no hard and fast rules we have to follow other than to *be aware of what we are doing.*

Second, we have to remember that society has our women caught in this trap as well. Women are taught to wait for the knight in shining armor to ride up on his white horse and whisk them away to a castle on a hill where they will be treated like a princess and live happily ever after. Check out *their* fairytale stories and cartoons. While this is not the literal dream of all modern girls, elements of those stories are imbedded deep into their psyches. Agree with them or not, women accept or wrestle with those ideas and images, like the marriage proposal on one knee, the expensive ring, and a guy who will take care of them forever, for years, if not their entire lives. For our part, some of us guys *want* to be the knight riding up on that white horse.

Here's a piece of sad trivia to keep in mind: The Equal Rights Amendment to the Constitution—the amendment written to *give women equal rights* to men—never passed because *women didn't vote for it*. Enough of them believed equal rights to really mean equal responsibility and accountability—no more getting to be the princess on the pedestal—to leave that amendment it in the political dumpster, maybe for good. So don't be surprised when now and then your girlfriend's modern equal-rights sensibilities take a back seat to deeper, seemingly hard-wired traditional desires.

Even armed with this education, you may choose to ignore these lessons and take the chance that everything will work out fine (just as your woman may say it will). She may tell you I'm full of shit. She may assure you that you will not become one of the "yes, dear" men. (By the way, if *she* has to assure you of this, you're on your way there already). Why is this sad fate so likely for you? It's that love drug. And while you are busy thinking yourself so lucky for having her in your life, you forget how lucky she is to have you in hers. If you really think the deal is so uneven that she isn't as lucky to have you as you are to have her, you may as well get out now because there's *no way* your relationship is going to last.

This low self-esteem nonsense of "I'm so lucky she loves me" is why guys fail to write prenuptial agreements despite the hefty divorce rate. These guys become "yes, dear" husbands. When their wives come down off their love-drug high, they see a guy who doesn't even respect himself. She doesn't intend to become the overbearing, demanding wife from the old cartoons, but over time she begins treating her husband disrespectfully. But *he* kills off the relationship by allowing this to happen. When (and if) these guys finally do bust out, they look for their freedom in divorce. They're looking for their balls, planning to strap on a pair and hit the road.

Believe me, couples in love save themselves a lot of trouble, money, and heartache with premarital counseling. Any good therapist asks the heavy questions regarding money, free time, and sex and helps the couple to deal with them from the get-go. You want to stack the deck *in favor* of a successful marriage instead of hoping not to have a bad one. Keep in mind that the *divorce laws are stacked against men*. Talk to any divorce lawyer and hear horror stories about guy after guy who lost his hard-earned house, half his assets and future income to the woman he once thought was the "girl of my dreams." In the stories, the "perfect girl" (which wasn't true either) turned into her evil twin: critical, demanding, and impossible to please. She may even have cheated on him—but she'll still get her half of everything and more—plus at least shared custody of the kids. I'm not saying the guy is the victim here; it takes two people to screw up a marriage. But once the chips are on the table, the wife tends to walk away the material winner.

The high you get from being in love will change sooner or later. If both people made good choices and *both are willing to work on the relationship*, the love can evolve into something really special and satisfying. We've all seen couples that have been together "forever" and are still in love. It happens. But even for them, that initial "love high" fades and they experience some rough times before they get the big prize of a happy, long-lasting relationship that they know how to maintain. For everyone else, the relationship eventually turns sour. The couple either breaks up, or if they stay together ("for the kids"), they settle in, sadly, to a bland loveless existence.

How do you avoid such a horrible fate? You want to be one of the cute old couples holding hands on the beach, still laughing, and when no one's looking, doing a little ass grabbing, don't you? I sure do. Talk to these old guys and listen to their advice. The really happy ones talk about learning to compromise, but their compromises are conscious ones. They decide what they can and cannot live with in their partners and they aren't afraid to tell their wives the truth. In short, the happy old guys are Men with Balls.

Be careful about accepting the advice of the older guys who warn you that you'll have to accept women "the way they are." Maybe they have accepted their wives the way they are just the way their wives have come to accept them. If so, that's fine. That couple has come to an understanding. But the old guys who say you have to keep working on making your wife happy because "if she's happy, you're happy," well; they have long ago given up on standing up for themselves. Comedians have endless bits about these guys because there are so many of them at every age. These are the "yes, dear" guys who expect you to live in your marriage like they lived in theirs.

Ball-less.

This can be confusing because some of these guys had massive balls in their jobs or other parts of their lives. But when they came home, they left their balls outside the front door. You look at them and can't understand why they let themselves be so powerless at home. Maybe their big balls at work made up for them being "yes, dear" guys at home. Who knows? But that's their problem. It doesn't need to be yours.

CHAPTER TEN

Worthwhile Women

Since I've been making references to Worthwhile Women throughout the book, some of you, perhaps the female readers (hi there) have jumped ahead to this chapter. The title *Worthwhile Women* might seem a little cold. Am I implying that there are girls and women who are not worth your time and energy no matter how good they look (or how available they are for sex)? Yes, I am. You can judge whether or not I'm being fair to women in general here, but there *are* (girls and) women who will prove to be nothing but trouble to you if you pursue them—*especially* if you are just out to get laid. Any older, experienced man will confirm this for you. Most of us learned the hard way after letting our little heads make a few ill-advised dating decisions.

Since you know what you want in your relationships with women more than I do, the "Worthwhile Woman" criteria are yours alone to set. Since *Growing Balls* is aimed primarily at young men, what makes a girl worthwhile to a fifteen-year-old boy *should* differ somewhat from what makes a woman worthwhile to a grown man ten years older or more. However, there are some aspects of women that any guy should look for, no matter what his age. Since I'm writing the book, here are my two cents on the subject.

Profile of a Worthwhile Woman

A Worthwhile Woman:

1. looks good enough to turn you on
2. has reasonable self-esteem
3. has interests that don't include you;
4. is willing to confront you on your bullshit—but does so respectfully
5. can handle being respectfully confronted on *her* bullshit
6. generally has a positive attitude about life
7. has a sense of humor.

Let's take these one at a time.

A Worthwhile Woman looks good enough to turn you on.

Since nearly every man's criteria for a Worthwhile Women includes at least *some* element of physical attraction, let's cover that now. In discussing this topic with a buddy, I was asked to emphasize that *we men are animals.* All animals have in-bred priorities, starting with the basic needs (food, shelter, sex). My buddy pointed out that we are driven by our animal natures to think and act in certain ways. We know what looks good to us. We know what we like. We know what we want.

You shouldn't be surprised about this, or ashamed. He's not making a case for a legal sexual free-for-all for men with any woman just because we get turned on and horny. Getting a sexual itch involving another person doesn't mean we have the right to scratch it. But we don't have to feel guilty about wanting to, either. We can acknowledge our animal natures without indulging them at the expense of others. Nonetheless, here's the bottom line: When it comes to women, looks matter to us.

Consider this: The deepest, healthiest, and longest-lasting marriages can start out with the guy's initial observation, "She's got a nice ass." This isn't rocket science, right? Women know this is true. Next time you go to a nice social gathering, take a look around at the women (like you wouldn't already). They certainly aren't dressing for comfort; not in those shoes, not in some of those outfits. The hair and makeup alone can take some women hours to "get right." Women have long suffered the discomfort of dressing to look good. If they were dressing for comfort, they'd be wearing faded coveralls and cheap flip-flops most of the time. And ironically, most men wouldn't care. We'd lust after them anyway. When I was in college, the most beautiful woman on campus regularly dressed in just that frumpy outfit—I suppose to deflect unwanted attention—and still, whenever she entered a room, both men and women's heads alike whipped around like lawn sprinklers and slowly followed her across the room. Meanwhile, a good man, a Man with Balls, will come to appreciate a woman's deeper qualities over time. But in the beginning, he's looking her over.

The fashion industry is driven by the fact that looks count, and advertising reinforces that notion. (By the way, dude, girls and women are looking *you* over too, so ignore your personal hygiene and current fashion trends at your own risk.) By making themselves attractive before leaving the house, women are not placing their *only* value in their looks. They say they want to look good for themselves, and that's probably true. They want to look good to other women too (but no, not for the reasons you hope, you dog). Women can be competitive with each other. But when all is said and done, women who pay attention to their looks recognize the truth that *looks matter to men*. For some of us, they mean everything; for others, just a little. Most of us are somewhere in the middle, but for all of us, they mean something.

Some of us set ridiculously high standards for looks. If you believe your girl has to look like she qualifies for *PLAYBOY* then you won't have many options for dating—most girls don't look that way. Does she have to have big breasts and a board-flat stomach? Have any dating criteria you want, but you have to live with the results of your own screening-out process. Meanwhile, if you *are* this type of guy, ask yourself why physical perfection is your standard for what makes a girl or woman "worthwhile." Chances are, that big ego of yours is probably causing you other problems too.

To sum up the question of attraction: Flexibility in the area of looks is helpful. Remember: The kinds of qualities that make a woman a great partner take longer to identify than her facial features, bra cup size, or measurements.

On the other hand, no matter what your standards are for looks, you need to be attracted to someone you're considering as a candidate for a long-term partner—and make sure she's attracted to you. For a man or a woman, it is unfair and just plain wrong to marry someone who doesn't turn you on. There are both men and women who are more interested in being taken care of in a marriage than in being a real partner. Couples have to be up front with each other about those kinds of expectations; otherwise, somebody in that relationship is going to feel cheated. If both spouses are expected to "forsake all others" during the marriage—in other words, don't cheat—then both partners have a responsibility to take care of themselves physically and be good sexual partners. A therapist I had years ago told me that "sex is 10 percent of a good marriage and 90 percent of a bad one." That's a good statistic to keep in mind.

So much for physical attraction. Let's move on.

A Worthwhile Woman has reasonable self-esteem.
The key word here is *reasonable*. *All* young people have some insecurity and teenaged girls will generally have less self-esteem than their older sisters. Put it this way: If the sixteen-year-old girl you're hot for can't make it through the day without either having an anxiety attack, trolling you or her friends for compliments, or jamming her finger down her throat to throw up her lunch to stay thin, then she's definitely questionable dating material. On the other hand, it's normal for a teenaged girl to worry about how she looks and whether or not people like her. How she handles her anxiety tells you how healthy she is. Walking basket cases make for problematic girlfriends and miserable wives.

When we're young—into our mid-twenties—we're busy developing our identities and deciding what kind of people we want to be. We're not fully baked yet, so some insecurity makes sense. However, a Worthwhile Woman, in general, actually likes at least some things about herself. She has her good and bad days; she has her "issues" to work on (like you do). Maybe she can be a bit of a drama queen now and then, but generally, she is pretty stable. She is okay with her own process of growing up. In this way, a girl growing into a Worthwhile Woman is like a guy who is finding and growing his balls. She's not matured yet but she is on her way. She's worthwhile to date *because* she is on her path to maturity.

Most Worthwhile Women have had some experience with Bad Boys. They get caught up in the attraction for a while, but older and wiser now, they are attracted to Men with Balls. Worthwhile Women know the difference, having learned the hard way about Bad Boys the same way guys, thinking with the little head, learned the hard way about too-easy or too-needy girls.

The last thing you want for a partner is a weak, insecure woman—not yet on her path to maturity—in search of a man to rescue her from her miserable life. If you're one of those guys who have to be the knight in shining armor, you'll latch on to this kind of women time after time. There are lots of girls and women out there looking for you to ride up and rescue them. Until a woman develops some reasonable self-esteem, she's going to *need you more than she wants you*. By now, we should all be clear that this is a recipe for disaster. In a healthy relationship, desire should generally outweigh need. Her insecurity will make her anxious, which she'll turn into controlling behaviors. And I'm talking about behaviors meant to control *you*. Her neediness, insecurity, and jealousy will make you nuts. Moreover, she'll resent you and hate herself for needing you too much. I just can't tell you what a drag it is to be in a relationship with a girl/woman like this.

Let me break this down in simple terms. There are two kinds of women with low self-esteem. The first kind tends to be very critical and very bitchy. It is *impossible* to change her miserable attitude or self-image by being nice or attentive to her. She'll see you as a wimp and walk all over you. You'll *never* turn her around by being good to her. Trust me on this. In fact, doing this will have just the opposite effect. This kind of woman *knows* she's being a bitch. Even if she "has a good heart" in there somewhere, she just can't seem to help herself or control this negative behavior. She knows she doesn't deserve to be treated as well as you are treating her, and so she won't respect you. She'll end up using you like a chump and then go off with a Bad Boy who treats her like crap. Why? *That's how she believes she deserves to be treated.*

The second type of insecure woman comes across as passive and weak. *Caution:* You *must* use the big head (the one on your shoulders) to avoid getting involved with these women. Why? These women are like sexual targets. They're often *way too easy* to get into bed—or at least they seem that way. These girls and women either don't know or forget that they have more to offer men than their sex appeal, so they focus on connecting with our little heads instead of connecting with our big ones.

Why is this a problem? After the little head is satisfied, the big one eventually wakes up. The big head knows that sex alone—no matter how much fun at the moment—doesn't make for much of a relationship. By the time these girls become women, they will have been sweet-talked or Bad-Boy'd into bed many times over by guys who just use them for sex and then dump them. They feel victimized and embittered by the experience. At some point, they either give up on relationships or fight back and get mean. When the latter happens, watch out. These women start to see *all guys* as predators—that means you, too—no matter if you're like that or not. If you have some of that white knight" stuff in you, if you're the rescuer type ("I'll show her that some guys are good"), then you're in for a bumpy ride with her that rarely works out well.

A Worthwhile Woman has interests that don't involve you.

A new relationship usually involves intensive time together, and that's fine. But soon enough, the rest of your life calls for your attention: school, work, friends, family responsibilities, creative projects, and so on. *You want the same to be true of your woman*, otherwise, you're in big trouble. She'll have nothing better to do than plan your schedule and make it revolve around her. That's a big red flag—ignore it at your own risk. If she can't let you get on with your interests and responsibilities, you might as well bail out now. She's going to weigh you down like an anchor and you'll soon be figuring out ways to dump her. By the same token, if you can't handle her continuing her interests and activities without you, then *you* are the problem. A Worthwhile Woman is going to look for ways to dump you—and rightly so.

A Worthwhile Woman will confront you when you're full of shit. And she'll handle it when you have to confront her for the same reason.

We all make fools of ourselves now and again. That's part of growing up. If you don't take risks, you don't gain experience. You should look for a partner who is brave enough to be honest with you. A Worthwhile Woman is going to tell you the truth, as she sees it. She won't let you make the same dumb mistakes over and over without at least trying to help you out with her perspective, even if she knows you might be mad at her for pointing out what an idiot you've been. Keep in mind that, most likely, you have also embarrassed her. Your behavior reflects on her, like it or not. The same holds true for when she screws up and subsequently embarrasses you. You have to be able to support one another, even when one of you is at your worst.

There are acceptable and unacceptable ways of confronting one another. A woman whose style of honesty is to put you down, especially in front of other people, is not worthwhile, not in my book (sic). If she puts you down publicly, she should be dumped—immediately. This behavior should not be tolerated. The only way a relationship should survive that sort of episode is if after being on the receiving end of an intense (and private) confrontation by you in return she admits being out of line and apologizes. In that case, you *can* give her a second chance. But if she does it again, save yourself the trouble. This is going to happen over and over. Break up. It's kind of like domestic violence, the pattern of men hitting women. A battered woman who thinks her man is going to stop just because he apologizes later is fooling herself. I'm not writing an advice book for women, but if I were, I'd give the same advice to them. Don't allow yourself to be publicly humiliated by anyone.

If you are married to this type of woman, you better get a *full commitment* from her to stop this type of behavior after it happens the first time. Even if she puts you down disrespectfully in private, or at home in front of your kids, remember that they are listening and watching for your reaction. You don't want to be an unhealthy role model that screws up *their* future notions of what makes an acceptable relationship.

A Worthwhile Woman generally has a positive attitude. She sees the glass as half full, not half empty; or at the very least, she sees half a glass of water.

This is a quality in a person you don't pick up by watching her from across the room. You figure this out from talking to a girl and getting to know her. An appreciative "Life is good" attitude in a partner is vital. She'll be much more fun and energizing to be around than a woman with a negative I'm-a-victim type attitude.

We all get into negative moods now and then, so don't judge her too quickly. Everybody is entitled to have bad days and the bleak attitudes they bring. But if a woman is always complaining about life being unfair and a struggle, wish her good luck and take off. Seriously. This can be hard to do, especially if you care about her. Also, you run the risk of proving her right by leaving her. What she doesn't realize is that she is creating her own reality. She believes men will leave her, so she acts in such a way as to make it happen. It's a sad but common process. Even if it makes you look like the bad guy, you have to go anyway. Your friends will support you.

If you do stay with her, one of two things will happen. Either she'll make a sudden and dramatic change for the better (it's possible, but do you *really* think that will happen?), or more likely, she'll bring you down and break your spirit. It's much harder to develop a positive attitude than it is to slowly slide into a negative one.

Unable to save her by getting her to see the lighter side of life, (try as you might), you'll likely end up drowning with her if you stay together. Why? Couples need to be more or less on the same page when it comes to an outlook on life. Just to have something in common, you'll come to see life the same way she does. You have seen this in other people, haven't you? Someone you know very well gets into a bad relationship and slowly undergoes a personality change; they don't notice it in themselves but you do.

Go for the girl who can celebrate life's victories as well as she deals with its inevitable struggles. She's a Worthwhile Woman or a girl on her way to becoming one.

A Worthwhile Woman has a good sense of humor.

This doesn't mean she has to laugh at all the same things you think are funny. But she has to find humor in life. It helps if you can make each other laugh. If you stay together, there will be plenty of stresses, disappointments, and tragedies in your lives—like there are for the rest of us. It's best to share with your mate an ability to find some humor in the darker times to remind you that they, too, will pass. After being in a negative relationship, finding a Worthwhile Woman is like a taking a breath of fresh air. Insist on a Worthwhile Woman for yourself and help your buddies to not settle for anything less.

CHAPTER ELEVEN

Your Buddies

I was about ten years old when my grandfather told me the following: "If a man, at the end of his life, can name five real friends, he should consider himself lucky." I had been telling him stories about my friends and me when he interrupted with this puzzling remark, effectively bringing my storytelling to a grinding halt. There seemed to be a criticism of me in there but I couldn't tell quite where. I do, however, remember feeling confused. I mean, I could name more than five friends in my fifth grade class alone, never mind buddies from the neighborhood, my religious youth group, or my Little League team. After all, friendships, for most kids, especially little kids, are simple. You size up the other kid, checking for obvious signs of weirdness, and once satisfied, just start playing. If all goes well, *boom*—you've made a friend. If someone says or does something mean or too weird, well, the friendship is over. Easy come, easy go.

I guess my grandfather felt I was throwing around the term "friend" pretty loosely, as kids will do, and he was reacting to me from a perspective a kid can't understand, as older folks will. Now that I'm in my mid-forties, however, I have a better sense of what the old man was trying to say. Real friendships are rare and precious, but it's unreasonable for a ten-year-old or even a young man to grasp this idea fully. For that, you need some life experience. Given grandpa's good intentions, his point shouldn't rot on the vine because of a clumsy presentation. So, being in between your age and his, I'll take a crack at fleshing out his point and making sense of it, from your perspective as a young man.

The truth? Most, if not all, of your current friendships will not stand the test of time. They won't last. Why? Because at your age you're experimenting with friendships like you do with other relationships—just like you're supposed to do. What works as a friendship today won't necessarily meet your needs in the future. Put it this way: Most of your present friendships won't last for the same reason you're not likely to marry the first girl you kiss or take to bed. Some guys get lost in that great flush of new love and end up marrying their first girlfriends—but not many—and those marriages rarely last. By getting to know a variety of women over time, a guy figures out what he is looking for in a life mate.

It is the same with friendships. Friendships are relationships—without the complication of romance. You meet someone and find you share some of the same interests. You enjoy talking together and decide to start hanging out and doing some things. You become friends. Then soon enough other factors enter the picture. Busy schedules get in the way of making plans. To make the best use of your limited play time, you meet one another's friends and try to mix with those groups. Maybe you fit in with the new group, maybe you don't. It is the same for them with your friends. Maybe they like him, maybe they don't. Along the way, people may get jealous or end up with hurt feelings. Why? Life is complicated and so are friendships.

Friendship is *important*. With friends we share our triumphs and failures. We get and give advice. We forgive and ask forgiveness from our friends. We can't fool them because they know better; they know *us* and usually much better than we think they do. If they don't know us, it's on us for holding ourselves back from them.

A man without friends is too scared to let himself be known by others. Exactly what he is afraid of depends on the man. Some men cover their insecurity with a gruff "I don't need anybody" exterior. That's bullshit. A man who has withdrawn into himself to the virtual exclusion of others is scared. I'm not talking about men who, in terms of personal style, prefer to be alone much of the time but still have a few friendships they keep up. Some men are less social than others; that's no big deal. But a man without friends at all is missing the basic social skills he needs to participate in friendships—which is sad when true—or he has no balls. Too scared to risk the potential rejection of trying to make a friend and then failing, he stays to himself and misses out on the obvious benefits of real friendship.

Friendships add meaning to our lives. The ties that bind us to friends make us stronger, better people. Even when friendships fall apart—which some inevitably do—we are better for the experience. There are lessons for us in the breakup that we take with us into the next friendship. We learn to be patient, to build trust slowly because it's foolish to trust too early in any relationship. A real friendship has weathered a few rough spots, including even a perceived (or real) betrayal here or there. There may even be the occasional separation— time away from each other to think, stew, or calm down after a fight. Whatever it takes. Friendships are like marriages—they take work but offer big payoffs to those who hang in there for the long haul.

So, let's say we can agree that friendships are important. Now let's look at types of friendships, because friendship means different things to different people. As a young man, you and your boys may see friendship in a simple "We've got each other's back" sort of way. You'll stand up for your buddies no matter what. Which sounds good, on the surface, but what about when your buddy is doing wrong? Are you disloyal if you won't stand by his side then? How about when he is making a mistake? What do you do then? He's riding blindly toward a cliff that you can see and he cannot. What kind of friend are you if you won't yell out a warning? Are you too scared of losing his friendship to tell him the truth?

I'm not suggesting you have to preach morals to your friends. Half the times we think our friends are on the wrong path it is *us* who are mistaken. But a friend will check out his concerns—respectfully, even reluctantly. Now and then, being a friend to another man feels more like a responsibility than a pleasure. It takes balls to say what needs to be said, especially if it looks like doing so may cost you the friendship. With luck, the friend who rejects you will come around, in time, after looking at his own behavior. He may end up confronting you back—then it will be *you* doing the soul searching. But that's what happens in friendships. That's the price you pay for doing the right thing.

Some old folks can tell you they met their best friend "way back when" and they are still friends today—but not many. If you grow up and live your life in the same town or area, your chances are better of holding on to your childhood friendships. But for the rest of us, our lives take too many unexpected twists and turns. Even people we met as kids who *could* make great life-long friends rarely do. Focusing on growing up and day-to-day activities, we lose track of one another. By the time you are in your forties, you will be lucky to even be in touch with a small handful of buddies from high school, college, the military, or wherever else you made strong connections with other guys. It doesn't mean you don't like each other anymore or have stopped caring. Your lives just move on. This is sad, but normal.

Though my grandfather didn't (or couldn't) explain what he meant by a "real friend," I think he meant the kind of friendship that stands up to the tests of time and stress. He meant the friendships that survive the arguments and undeserved blowups that happen when friends take their anger out on each other. I think he was talking about friends who own up to their mistakes, apologize and mean it; friends who stand by you in triumph and tragedy. Those friendships are rare. Sometimes real friendships need to take lengthy breaks apart while feelings mend from run-ins. Sometimes friends need time to gain some perspective.

At your age, guys let girls get in the way of close friendships. Girls do the same thing with their friends. When you get older, moves and career choices are more likely to get in the way. But your real friendships, they survive. After a long absence, real friends pick up right where they left off.

So, when you're on your deathbed someday, will you be able to count five real friends you have had in your life? Will I? Perhaps more importantly, will *our* names be on the lists of other guys when they are counting *their* real friends? That will depend on the kind of friends we are to them. Maybe my grandfather was aiming a little low with the five-friend figure. I don't know, and frankly, I don't want to get caught up in a game of numbers. But I can appreciate his point, if not his delivery. So let's focus now for a bit on what real friendship is.

A real friend tells you a painful truth even if it means risking the friendship.
Despite what young men tend to think, friendship is not just "having each other's back." In this way of thinking, you are expected to lie to protect your friend from the consequences of his mistakes or bad judgment. You're supposed to take his side when you know he's wrong.

That isn't friendship. That is shared weakness—having no balls, together.

Guys like this—bullies, for example—will hang out in packs, sticking together because of an unspoken agreement: No one confronts any one else on their antisocial behavior. And together they'll attack anyone else who does. Again, this isn't friendship. Neither is letting your buddy borrow your apartment so he can cheat on his wife or girlfriend. Try encouraging him to grow some balls and act with integrity—make a decision and live with it. That's friendship. I'm not saying you should become your friend's mother or Sunday school teacher. I'm suggesting you support him in his integrity instead of his dishonesty.

What else is friendship about? When you keep making the same mistake and can't (or won't) see the pattern, you need a real friend to spell it out for you. Here are a few situations where it helps to have some real friends.

1. You see your friend's drinking becoming a problem for him and you're getting worried. Tell him the truth: "I'm worried about you. I think you're drinking too much."

2. Your friend is about to marry a woman who treats him badly. She nags him about his time spent with friends. She puts him down in front of other people and takes advantage of him. He complains about her and looks unhappy much of the time but here he is, ready to marry her. You say, "I know I'm supposed to be happy for you but I'm not. I'm worried that you're making a mistake."

3. Your friend is looking bad. Maybe he's lost his sense of humor and seems down. He may be gaining or losing weight. He's complaining a lot but isn't doing anything about it. He isn't making any changes. You say, "You're not looking or acting like yourself lately. What's the story? Are you okay?" A real friend is curious and will listen to the answer. Maybe he'll offer some support.

4. Your friend complains he's not getting the attention he thinks he deserves (at work, home, school, on the team, in his relationship, etc.) but he's acting like a victim. He's not seeing the part he plays in his problems and just bitches about everyone else. After acknowledging his frustration, you say, "I hear you're blaming everyone else, but what's your part in all this? Is this really everyone else's fault?"

There are so many reasons you might end up telling a friend "You're not being honest with yourself" that there's no point in writing more examples.

Does all this sound harsh? Unrealistic? Are these things *wrong* to say just because they would be *hard* to say? Don't walk in the door and say, "Hey, dude, you know that work situation you're always bitching about? Well, you know what? You're completely full of shit. And as far as I can see, it's all your own fault."

No, that's not likely to fly very well. You ought to warm a guy up a little before saying that sort of thing. Besides choosing your words a little more carefully, use your judgment and pick the right moment to drop bombs like these. But when you say them out of friendship, you're challenging and protecting your buddy. Polite society tells us to soft-peddle the truth or not say it at all. According to this wholly bullshit thinking, you're somehow a better friend if you stand there watching while your buddy bloodies himself against a brick wall again and again rather than face him with the truth as you see it.

We have all done this. We've sat back and watched while people we cared about made mistakes. How do we excuse our wimpy behavior? "Well, I saw this coming and I guess I *could* have warned him—*but he never asked me for my opinion.*" Or "*I didn't think it was any of my business.*" So you're off the hook? Just like that? Is that really the position you want *your* friends to take as they stand by watching you make the same painful mistakes again and again? I don't think so.

Why is this kind of behavior considered friendship? Perhaps more to the point, why are we supposed to pretend we're *not* judging our friends' behaviors? Because we are. You do too. Come on now, be serious. We make judgments about people all the time, *especially* the people we care about. We may not talk out loud about those judgments, but we make them. And when we talk to other people about those judgments, that's gossip. That's right. We're not proud of it but we guys gossip too when we don't tell our friends *to their faces* what we are thinking and feeling. Any fourth-grader will tell you there is nothing more damaging to a friendship than gossip. Your urge to gossip should be a red flag for you—a signal that there is something important to tell your friend, but you're either too afraid to follow through or this person isn't really your friend.

This isn't about being a nosy jerk or a know-it-all who is always minding other people's business. This is about being someone's friend—a real friend—and having the balls to tell him the truth as you see it when you believe you need to do so. Now mind you, I'm talking about *the important issues* here, not differences in opinion or taste, the small stuff that don't really matter. It's easy to tell a guy his shirt and pants don't match—and he's likely to accept that feedback easier than hearing you say his fiancée reminds you of a bad-tempered prison guard with a chip on her shoulder.

Which brings up an obvious point: When you put yourself on the line and speak up, you may end up being completely wrong—after all, you probably don't have all the facts. (Like maybe he *likes* women who act like bad-tempered prison guards.) That's embarrassing but okay; being right isn't the point of speaking up. What matters is that, as a real friend, you cared enough to say what you are thinking and feeling—because you thought it might help in an important situation. Your truth may not be *the* truth. In cases like these, it's usually a relief to be wrong. You can and probably should start off by admitting you may be completely wrong about what you're about to say. When you *are* wrong, you have to hope your friend will be able appreciate your intentions even if he feels stung or insulted in the moment.

I'd like to think that my grandfather chose five as the magic number of a lifetime's real friends because he knew that most people we consider our friends will *not* risk telling us the truth about ourselves. It's not that they don't care; they just aren't willing to pay the potentially high price. You know what I mean. Face it: When addressing the tough topics, you risk being told to "mind your own fucking business." You also risk the friendship itself.

But if you're not willing to risk these things, don't plan on being on this person's deathbed list of friends. You might not have made it anyway, but you won't even deserve consideration if you weren't honest about the important things.

As for me, I don't buy the "five friends" theory. I think I can do better than that, but it will mean some regular and honest checking to make sure I've held on to my balls.

CHAPTER TWELVE

Knowing That You're Ready

If you've bought into the idea that you shouldn't commit yourself to any woman, even a Worthwhile Woman before you're ready, the natural question eventually becomes, "Okay, so how do I know when I *am* ready?" There are different answers to that question, with much depending on:

1. who is asking it (guys operate on different schedules) and
2. the kind of relationship and commitment you're thinking of making.

Some commitments are much heavier than others, right? For example, from our *Growing Balls* perspective, we wouldn't equate a sixteen-year-old's agreement to "go out" (go steady) with a girl with a twenty-year-old's decision to get engaged or a twenty-two year-old man's agreement to have kids.

It is the husband-and-father commitments that concern me most, so here is a test you can give yourself to assess your readiness for the role of husband. We'll look at the father role after that. Like the last test on getting loaded, this test also has no black-and-white scoring scales that should absolutely determine a guy's decision one way or the other. But if you answer the questions honestly, you'll know the right thing to do. Then the only question remaining will be

"Will you listen to yourself and follow through on what you now know to be right?"

Test Number Two: Your Readiness to be a Husband

1. **Whose idea is it to get engaged? (circle one)**

Hers Mine We decided together

This is an important question. What or who is driving the decision to get married? I have seen high school sweethearts hurry to get engaged and married before one of them leaves for college or the military, out of fear that otherwise the relationship may not survive the separation (and truthfully, the odds say it probably would not). To the loving couple, however, this feels romantic. But their decision is driven much more by fear than by love. Fear is a *terrible* motivation for marriage—fear that you won't find anyone better, fear of being alone, fear of being "left behind," fear of hurting someone, fear of what others might think about you. These and other fears can invade your thoughts and affect your ability to make a good decision. Fear can grab you by the balls. Don't let it. Remember: The divorce rate tops 50 percent. The percentage of happy marriages that start from fear is *very* low. Don't believe me? Ask around.

Here's an easy way to know if fear is driving your marriage plans. If you and your girl used the phrase "What if . . . ?" in making the decision to get married, your engagement is based on fear. Need an example? Here's one. A young couple just graduating from high school is faced with the following dilemma. The guy is offered a full scholarship—room, board, and tuition—to a great college a thousand miles away. It's a once-in-a-lifetime opportunity. But they both can't go. His other choice is a local community college that they can afford and attend together. During the painful discussion that follows the scholarship offer, his sweet and beautiful girl asks him, with pleading eyes, "What if one of us meets someone else while we're apart?"

This is an easy question to answer. They'll probably break up. I know this sounds a little cold, but it's the truth and she knows it. So does he. If he takes the scholarship, the relationship probably won't last. Why? Their needs and desires don't match. After he leaves, his girl, at some point, will be angry with him for leaving. There's a good chance that she will meet someone else and get married—because in truth, she wanted a husband (and to be a wife) more than she wanted her boyfriend.

If it's really him she wants, she'll wait for him. But that might turn out to be a bad idea because while he's at college, even though her guy will try to be true to her—at least for a while—he's going to meet other women, and he will discover that they're pretty cool too. They're fun and interesting—and hot, and think the same of him. The girl he thought was the "only one" for him turns out to be one of *many* possible women with whom he could be happy. This comes as a shock to him. What else does he learn? He learns that he really isn't ready to settle down after all, which he probably knew deep inside but couldn't admit to himself, let alone to his girlfriend—and is probably why he accepted the scholarship in the first place. This is the scenario the young couple fears when they ask "What if . . . ?"

So, more often than not, what happens? Fearful of losing her to another guy or fearful of "breaking her heart," he declines the scholarship. They get married. Maybe they have a long-lasting and happy marriage; maybe they don't. But think of it this way: If they "are meant" to be together (whatever that means), they *will* end up together. So in the meantime, if you are the guy, why not go on and get the advantages of a great free education, plus all the experiences of being a man on your own for four years? If the relationship is so good, the couple should show some faith in it. The same goes for a guy who is entering the military or taking a job in another place.

Is turning your back on such opportunities necessarily such a bad idea? After all, there is no guarantee of happiness no matter what path is chosen. Each decision will bring a life with both pain and pleasures. But if this guy turns his back on a great opportunity out of fear, he will always know his decision was ball-less.

So while we're on the subject of fear, consider this. If you're harboring serious doubts about getting married, don't do it. Just say no. You're not ready. I'm not talking about pre-wedding jitters. Those are normal. Most marriages, even good ones, start with the bride and/or groom having moments of "What the hell am I doing?" panic the night before the ceremony. That's why you're supposed to have your best friend by your side all the way to the altar. Your best man should be willing to be honest with you, hopefully long before you rent the tux, let alone on the limo ride to the ceremony. Frankly, you should be talking with this guy before you even propose.

2. Is there pressure on the two of you to get married? *Yes No I don't know*

    a. If yes, who is pressuring you? _____

    b. Why? _____

There are all sorts of pressures to consider here. Sometimes parents or friends put on the pressure. Sometimes it's fear, like from question number one. You may be thinking: All my friends are getting married. I might as well too. Well, trust me. These are *not* good reasons for getting married. Save "Why not?" and "What the heck?" for less important decisions. Is your girlfriend pressuring you? Is she threatening to leave you if you don't marry her? That's *very* common, my young friend, and we've covered that in previous chapters. Fall for that threat and you're really screwed. Good marriages don't start with threats, or obligations.

Obligations? That's a tough word, isn't it? For example, if you're getting engaged because you've accidentally gotten your girlfriend pregnant, the two of you have some serious thinking to do. Certainly, some couples do great from this starting position. But in general, they don't. It's a particularly difficult way to start a marriage, and I don't recommend it. Also, in this day and age, I can't really buy the notion of an "accidental pregnancy" because let's face it, buddy, birth control ain't rocket science. No method is fool proof, I know, but two horny people who don't want to become parents can pretty much avoid this painful ethical and moral situation. If your girl got pregnant, chances are somebody here hasn't been completely honest—or careful—and dishonesty about something this important is a poison pill to a new marriage. Meanwhile, the tough alternatives are abortion or adoption, both tough choices—and I'm sorry, but I can't help you there. You two are going to need some unbiased counseling to make that decision. Better to avoid that situation from the start.

Finally, if you've saved your virginity for marriage, the pressure to tie the knot may be coming from your little head. Remember that thinking with your dick is a dangerous proposition and letting the little head overrule the big one is always a mistake. In your parents' and grandparents' generations, and countless ones before that, a large percentage of marriages got started with at least one, if not both, partners entering the marriage bed with their virginity intact. That is a personal option you can choose today, as well, but there is far more social support in your generation for exploring your sexuality before marriage. Many people think this is a bad thing and the pressure today to stay a virgin until marriage has mostly religious roots. If you can set aside the "fear of God" argument, you are left with more reasonable considerations regarding premarital sex that have already been covered in *Growing Balls*.

3. **How seriously do you take the concept of commitment in marriage?**

>   a. *Very seriously. It's 'til death do us part, no matter what.*
>   b. *Pretty Seriously. I'm in there for the long haul.*
>   c. *I love her and that's all that counts.*
>   d. *Dang, dude, back off and stop jammin' me up.*

Honestly, B is the only good answer. Sure, the typical marriage vows point to A so I understand if you chose it. I've been a licensed marriage and family therapist since 1989 and a married man for over twenty years, so believe me, I understand and support traditional concepts of commitment in marriage. But for any Man with Balls (and for any Worthwhile Woman), there *are* deal-breakers in any marriage. Violence and serious betrayal are simply not tolerable. If you chose C, your idealism is charming, but you haven't thought this through very well. Love *isn't* all that matters. Safety and integrity matter too. So does having some common interests, compatible temperaments, and so on. You can love a woman and still know you shouldn't marry her.

Commitments are best made with eyes wide open. That's why even a minister dressed as an Elvis impersonator in a cheesy Las Vegas wedding chapel—a guy who doesn't care if you're prepared or not—won't marry you and your girl if you guys show up drunk. You have to *at least* know what you are doing. So that answer, C, is for guys stoned beyond reason on a love high. They need to sober up a little before getting engaged, let alone married. As for answer D, okay, I'm being a wise-ass with that one. But I have heard versions of that answer from real guys, and if you think about it, anyone who chooses D is only a more extreme version of the guy who chooses C.

4. **How do you feel about yourself when you are with her?**

>   a. *Like the King of the World.*
>   b. *I like myself the same with or without her.*
>   c. *I feel lucky that she's choosing to be with me.*
>   d. *I wonder if I am good enough for her.*
>   e. *I haven't given this question much thought before.*
>   f. *What the hell kind of question is this?*

Be honest, now. Okay, A, B, C, and D are all normal and fine choices. If you chose one of these, depending on how you're feeling today, each of the other three are probably likely answers you would give on a different day. When you're knee deep in a love-drug high, you answer A. When you're feeling more level, you answer B. When you're maybe feeling less confident than usual, you might choose C or even D. The guys who chose E and F' on this question chose C and D, respectively, in question number three.

5. **How ready are you to be sexually faithful to one person?**

   a. *I've had enough experience to know I'm ready to settle down.*
   b. *We have this agreement, see, and while I don't plan to scam on her . . .*
   c. *I've had so much pussy I have to leave some for everybody else . . .*
   d. *Does that* have *to be one of the vows?*

Okay, so this is a no-brainer. But if you can't answer A you do have a problem. Some men lose their virginity to their wives and live happily ever after. That's great. Good for them. For everyone else, there is no set number of partners that defines how much sexual experience is *enough* for any particular guy.

Answer B is dicey. Good luck on that one. One question, though: Are you ready to have your wife play by the same rules? (I didn't think so.) Meanwhile, if you chose C, you're either full of shit or an A guy with attitude—which is cool. Balls and attitude go together just fine.

As for answer D, no, a promise to only have sex with each other from now on actually *doesn't* have to be one of the vows. It's between you and your betrothed; it's your marriage, so you two can do whatever you want. Y'all should keep in mind, however: *Very few* of these marriages work. Hardly any couples have no rules about sex with other people. Maybe if you're both porn stars, or plan to be a couple that "swings," *maybe* you guys can make it work. From what I know, even within the "swinging" subculture, couples have some rules about sex outside the marriage. If you're serious about this option, many books have been written on the topic so go read a few of them when you're done with *Growing Balls*. But you were probably kidding anyway, right?

6. **When you two argue, how good are you at making sure you get heard?**

   a. *We've never had an argument.*
   b. *I hang in there until I'm satisfied we've both had our say.*
   c. *Okay, I guess. We don't fight too much.*
   d. *I just let her talk until she's done. There's no point in arguing with her.*

Okay, first of all, A is a *huge* red flag. If you two really never argue—about anything—then either something is wrong or you haven't been together very long. Come on now: Couples *disagree* about things. They get frustrated with one another. I'm not saying you and your gal should go around the house yelling and screaming—and again, like we've covered already, violence is never okay. But fair fighting is healthy. Normal couples have disagreements, frustrations, and so on, and these *have* to be worked through somehow. As a therapist, I've seen plenty of couples that were too afraid to argue with each other; these people have weak relationships and are afraid of breaking up. But in twenty years of doing counseling and forty-eight years of life, I've *never* seen one where there wasn't anything to argue about.

Answer B? The best answer, hands down. You hang in there until you both feel satisfied that you've been heard. You may not solve any given problem in one sitting, but you can both be heard and understood by the other and agree to disagree before ending the argument for now. Here's a good marriage tip: Don't go to bed angry.

Answer C is okay, too. Some couples do argue less than others. As long you both stand up for yourselves, C is an acceptable answer, and frankly, you should consider yourself lucky to have hooked up with someone so compatible to yourself.

Now: If you chose the last answer, D, you have a *big* problem. Why is letting her "talk until she's done" without fighting back a bad thing? For one thing, it shows a major lack of balls on your part. You won't be able to keep that up for long without getting into sneaky paybacks of some sort, probably in weak, ball-less, passive-aggressive ways we have already covered in this book. Guys who act like this usually don't recognize the little shitty things they do as wrong. Why? They either can't see their own behaviors honestly, or they think their women "have it coming to them" for acting bitchy. So if you chose, D, wise up. Because you can't figure out how to make yourself understood in your relationship, you've given up trying. Is this what you plan to teach your son about and relationships and girls? Remember, if your girlfriend or wife "acts like a bitch" a lot of the time, you probably have as much to answer for as she does because you not only tolerate that behavior, you actually help create it. By not fighting back, you don't set any limits in the relationship. You don't let her know what is and is not tolerable to you and she cranks up her behavior trying to find that line.

This lame and ball-less strategy of letting your girl rag and nag you until she ends up looking, sounding (and feeling) like a bitch eventually backfires.

First of all, she's not going to change her behavior this way. She'll just start losing her self-respect for being bitchy, and she'll blame you for it. If you do stay together, you get to be married to a bitch who comes to hate herself *and* you. That's not what you want, is it? If she started out as a Worthwhile Woman and turned into a bitch with you, she'll eventually catch on to your ball-less game and her ugly response to it, retrieve her self-respect, and leave. And she should. For a Worthwhile Woman, falling into the "bitch" role is not okay.

I'm dead serious about this: Answering D is really one of the few deal-breakers on this test (along with serious betrayal or violence). It's a litmus test. If you chose D, you can conclude with confidence that you are not ready to be anyone's husband. Until you're willing and able to speak your mind, making yourself understood with clarity and dignity, you have no business getting married.

If you're convinced the relationship is worth saving, go see a marriage counselor before you tie the knot. You both will learn the communication skills you need to make the marriage work.

7. **How did you do on the "Do I Have a Problem?" drug/alcohol test?**

   a. *Aced it. I don't use at all.*
   b. *Fine. I'm pretty moderate.*
   c. *Okay. But I need to be careful when it comes to _____.*
   d. *Um, actually, not so good.*
   e. *Fuck you. I already have a mother.*

The first four answers are all good because they're honest, though D requires some work and changes in behavior. If you chose D, and especially E, you're not ready for a serious commitment to another person. Not yet. Why? Because no matter how great the woman is, you won't be able to get it together just to please or satisfy her. Anyone who has been down this road will tell you that sobriety is a personal journey. Try and get clean and sober for a woman and you'll just come to resent her. That is a change you have to make for yourself. You need to figure out how to get balanced, emotionally and physically, before you can connect well enough with another person to have a satisfying relationship. And although the question of readiness for fatherhood is the subject of the next test, while we're on the subject now, just ask anyone who was raised by an alcoholic or drug-addicted father to tell you about his or her childhood

8. What do you do to build or maintain your self-esteem?

    a. *I read. I stay on top of current events. I have well-reasoned opinions.*
    b. *I play sports and I'm always looking at ways to get better at my job.*
    c. *Hobbies. I'm always working on my skills. I like the challenge.*
    d. *My girlfriend makes me feel good about myself. So, sex, I guess.*
    e. *I don't worry much about it. I'm fine.*

Actually, all these answers can be okay. The weakest one is D, and not because there's anything wrong with letting your girl make you feel better. That's fine. You *should* be able to make one another feel good, and sex is a great part of it. The problem comes from *relying* on your partner to make you feel good about yourself. This puts you in a weak, too-needy position in the relationship.

Choosing E is okay for some guys, but for others it shows a lack of drive, passion, discipline, and motivation. As for the first three answers, some guys are more "in their heads" than others. They focus on their intellects for their self-esteem. Other guys are more into being physical. Their self-esteem comes from being in shape. Some guys get their self-esteem from working with their hands, doing art, playing music, building things, and so on.

The healthiest approach to building self-esteem includes elements of all three. I encourage all young men to exercise their minds as well as their bodies. *Growing Balls* is full of encouragements to pick up a hobby or two and get good at them. It's good for developing focus and discipline, and its fun (and useful) to have areas of expertise.

9. How do you handle your mistakes?

    a. *I 'fess up to whoever is affected by the mistake.*
    b. *I get pissed at myself and feel embarrassed or ashamed.*
    c. *I try and hide my mistakes and/or fix them before any one finds out.*
    d. *I realize that mistakes are how you learn, so while I'm not thrilled to make them, I'm not too hard on myself about them.*

Over the years I have chosen each of these answers, and now and again, they are all still true for me. I wish I could say I am *always* an A plus D, but I'm not. (I'll give myself an honest "usually.") My friends and I have determined that unless you can fix your mistake *before* it affects anyone else, it is best to just 'fess up, get it off your chest, and then work on a solution. This builds trust in your relationships and actually feels good once you get over the sting of admitting your screw-up. Assuming you had good intentions, a mistake is just that—a mistake. No one should beat you up for making mistakes—but they can expect you to learn from them. Your wife deserves a man who will learn from his mistakes. Your children deserve this, too, as do your colleagues and bosses. So it's best you develop the *attitude* from answer D.

Actually, you need to remember D is true even when you don't feel that way. Your mistakes will be embarrassing, and other people's mistakes can drive you nuts (for example, at work). In your marriage, your wife is going to make plenty of unpleasant mistakes and so will you. When the anger dies down, true forgiveness must follow or the relationship is doomed. I am not just talking about her forgiving you or you forgiving her. That's important too, but you learning how to forgive yourself for your mistakes is an absolute must. If you are not good at forgiving yourself (and others), you're going to make a lousy partner and parent. The same goes for your wife. People who can't forgive themselves for their mistakes tend to go through life by not facing up to them, making themselves and those who have to deal with them miserable. You know people like this. Self-forgiveness is a *huge* issue.

10. Have you grown your balls yet and do you know how to keep them?

I tried to make this a multiple-choice question like the others but I couldn't pull it off. How do you boil down to a few choices all the possible answers to this question? So let's consider this an essay question you have to answer to yourself.

By this point in *Growing Balls*, you should know what I'm asking. Are you living with integrity or not? Examine your morals and values, and not just the ones expected of you by parents, bosses, your religion, or the law. You may be living up to the expected values, whether or not they are actually yours. I'm talking about those morals and values that you really own. How are you doing in terms of living up to them? Your wife will naturally have a vested interest in you making good ball-based decisions. While you're single, your decisions are yours alone—not so for a married man.

If you have succeeded in choosing a Worthwhile Woman to marry, she's going to expect you to have some balls. This is a reasonable expectation. She's not demanding perfection (whatever that would mean), because if she were, she wouldn't qualify as a Worthwhile Woman. (Perfectionists make for *very* difficult partners.) But as for choosing a husband, this is the biggest decision of her life. She's picking you to be her life partner and the father of her children. She's looking for the whole package of what she believes a man should be— and she's looking for it in *you*, big guy. How do you feel about that? Ask yourself: Am I ready to be her husband?

*　　*　　*

CHAPTER THIRTEEN

Being a Family Man

What comes next is the money quiz, guys, what the whole rest of the book has been leading up to. Marriage is certainly an important commitment, and you *are* planning to take it seriously, right? But in the grand scheme of things, the marriage commitment *pales* next to the commitment of parenthood. You can always divorce your wife and go on to live separate lives—that's only sad and disappointing. But with little ones in the picture, it's another story altogether. The consequences for your kids are long term and profound if your marriage doesn't work. Even relatively smooth divorces (and how many of those are there?) are painful for everybody when there are children involved.

Unless you have had some honest conversations with your partner before you start making babies, you are risking blundering into the most important job you will ever have. As a Man with Balls, this is not what you want to do. So here are five tough questions for you and your partner to hash out together as you consider becoming parents.

Test Number Three: Your Readiness to be a Father

1. Are you two married?

> *a. Yes*
> *b. No*
> *c. We're engaged*
> *d. We're thinking about it*

This is where I'm glad not to be your counselor. If you two were in a professional relationship with me—marriage and family therapist to clients—I would have to follow some basic rules of the profession regarding giving you my opinion on questions like this. Instead of setting the agenda—my agenda—like I get to do with this book, my obligation would be to help you explore the issues that are important to you. With a question like this, the status of your relationship with the mother-to-be of your child, it would be unethical for me to foist my personal opinions onto you. Be careful with therapists who, because of their own biases or moral/religious perspectives, feel free to tell you what they think you should do.

This "hands off" stance sometimes frustrates clients who, facing tough decisions, just want to write their check and have the therapist "tell me what to do." But a therapist is in a very influential position and ethically must not take advantage of the situation to advance his or her own values. I have been on both sides of the couch: I know people have to make their own decisions in order to own the consequences of their actions.

However, thankfully, our relationship is strictly writer to reader, and *Growing Balls* is my soapbox, so I get to offer all the advice I want and you're free to reject any or all of it. No matter who wants to throw in their two cents of advice, when it comes to decision time, the only opinions that will matter are yours and your partner's.

Having said all that, let's get back to the question at hand. By now, you know my bias regarding parenting: Kids deserve to grow up with the attention of two loving, committed parents, and whenever possible, that's the way to go. If as a young man you are not married to your parent-partner-to-be, I have to ask: Why are you trying to make a baby now? If you have not made that commitment to one another, why take on the responsibility of parenthood now?

If you are just engaged, having a baby now means you're not going to give the marriage a chance to gel a bit before your new roles of husband and wife change to that of parents. Consider this: Your marriage deserves to have a life of its own for a while. With any luck, after the kids grow up and move away you two will still be married. It's important to have had a marriage relationship *without* children; it will be the foundation you return to once the kids take off on their own. It isn't mandatory to do this but it is a good idea. Many older couples are absolutely lost (and in fact get divorced) once their kids move out. It's good to think ahead.

Admittedly, a marriage certificate is no guarantee of a successful life-long marriage. Moreover, you can be married for years before having kids and still wind up divorced. It happens every day, right? On the other hand, you can decide *not* to get married (or not be allowed to by law, as is the case with gay couples) and still successfully raise a family. Lots of nontraditional families (single parents, unmarried straight couples, gay couples, and so on) do very well even though these families face challenges that the traditional "mom and dad" couples don't. However, for the sake of this test, I'm going to assume you are a straight man thinking of having a child with a straight woman.

The act of getting married—making a public declaration of your commitment to one another—does have significance, not to mention legal benefits. So while it isn't necessary to get married before having kids, you and your partner should be pretty clear about your family plans if you decide not to go that route. If you're "still thinking about getting married" you're probably not ready to be parents.

2. **How did you do on test number two? Are you ready to be a husband?**

   a. *There were no big surprises; I'm good to go.*
   b. *I'm ready. There are a few things I figure I should work on, but who doesn't have a few issues?*
   c. *My girlfriend says you're making this way too complicated. She wants me to stop reading this and look at Hawaiian honeymoon brochures . . .*
   d. *Does it really matter? I'll figure things out as I go along. That's what most people do, isn't it?*

By now, this should be a no-brainer. The first two answers are acceptable. Answer C means you have not yet located your balls. Besides which, you're not even married yet. (Go review question number one.) If she's trying to cut short your thinking process now it's because she's prepared and perfectly happy to do your thinking for you. As for answer D, ask yourself this: If your own father had taken this test before spawning you, is that the answer you would have wanted *him* to choose?

3. How would you describe your relationship with your own parents?

    a. We have (or had) a great relationship. I hope I do as good a job raising my kids as my folks did with me.

    b. I love my parents. They drive me a little nuts sometimes but it's generally good.

    c. My parents and I don't get along too well—I keep my contact with them to a minimum.

    d. My parents are/were a mess. I wouldn't let them near my kids.

This question is more important than it looks, and I have *lots* of comments on it. The right answer to this question? Any of them can be fine, although if D is true, that's sad. I hope you can choose between A or B because that implies you had at least a "good enough" relationship with your parents, and likely, a childhood with normal ups and downs.

The rest of my comments here are for those of you who had to choose C or D. These last two choices imply you probably had a tougher time growing up than most other guys, with varying degrees of problems from the "my parents were sort of crazy" to the extremes of abuse—physical, emotional, or sexual, or a combination of the three. Let's face it; some kids get stuck with terrible, abusive childhoods. It's not fair, of course, but the parents of these kids were most likely neglected or abused themselves as children and therefore not capable of being much better parents than were their own before them; those problems tend to get passed on from generation to generation.

What you need to know in figuring out if you are ready to become a dad yourself is this: whatever unresolved issues you have with your own parents and how they raised you—whether big or small—will be replayed in some way between you and your wife and you and your kids. This is true of all of us. This doesn't mean you will necessarily make the exact same mistakes with your kids that your parents made with you, but the old emotional baggage will affect your behavior as a husband and dad. This makes it important for you to make sense out of your parents' behaviors and attitudes and make some peace with how you were raised. This isn't easy and *most people don't do it.* They assume they'll *never* act like their parents did, and then, years later—and to their horror—they find themselves doing exactly that. That's when many people finally seek counseling.

Mental and emotional problems follow families through generation after generation from a wide variety of causes. Some problems come from the inside out (like mental disorders handed down through our genes) while others come from the outside in (responding to chronic stress or traumatic and terrible events like crime, war, abuse, and so on). A terrible event happening to one person in a family can have bad effects on generations to follow.

Here's a tough truth to swallow: people behave the way they do *because they are doing the best they can*, given their circumstances and limited skills and abilities. This is a good thing to remember when you're trying to forgive someone for hurtful behaviors. However, when the best a person can apparently do is still pretty bad, this truth can be *very* hard to swallow and rarely makes you feel much better. This is when you want to say (or scream), "Fine, but how I got treated still wasn't fair!"

This is also true.

It's hard to look at a dad who regularly gets drunk, shirks his family responsibilities, and hits his wife and kids, and then say about him, "Well, I guess he's doing his best." Wouldn't his *best* be sobriety and anger management? Why can't he communicate his anger with stern words rather than mean ones, or with words at all instead of fists?

Until this dad slows down on his drinking, or stops altogether, he won't be able to work on his social skills; nor will he get a grip on his temper. Until he takes a sober look at his unmet needs and the feelings they bring, he won't even know why he has a quick temper, let alone be able to control it. In other words, *under present circumstances*, he is *unable* to treat his family well. This isn't an excuse—but it is a fact. This is why domestic violence counselors encourage women who are not ready to leave their abusive husbands to have a safety plan for themselves and their kids including a safe (and secret) place to go, some saved money, and so on. They know his behavior is going to continue until he has other options. No amount of heartfelt apologizing is going to make up for him not knowing any other way of dealing with his feelings.

All of us have our shortcomings and limitations that, most often, don't end up causing misery in other people. Our friends and family accept us—including our sometimes weird ways—and we accept them. As long as we aren't dangerous or mean, the people who love us cut us slack. But we all know people whose personal problems *do* make others miserable. These are the abusive parents, the neighbors from hell, the power-tripping bosses, and the other people about whom we mutter "what an asshole" as we exit their presence. Their rotten behavior may drive us crazy and make us mad, but they really don't have the skills to do much better. This is confusing for healthier people who understand that life is better when people get along. Getting along means having friendships and being on good terms with others. Sounds good to you and me, right?

Well, being close to other people isn't so attractive to everyone. People who push others away with their attitudes and behaviors *can't handle closeness* so they avoid it, even with their own families. When we step back from being mad at what they do and say, we scan to see the bigger picture; and while we still hate their behavior, we can feel sad for the person.

As the expression goes, misery loves company. If we all have a need to feel understood by others, how does the miserable person get this need met? What is the "best" they can do? Easy: *They can make you feel as miserable as they feel.*

That's what I mean when I say people behave the way they do because they are doing the best they can, given their circumstances and abilities. True, they *can* change their circumstances and acquire new abilities if they are so motivated. That doesn't mean they will, though, right? I'm all for having high expectations of parents and holding them accountable for their behaviors. I also know that some people don't *want* to change. So, if your parents continue to display rotten, unsafe behaviors and are either not open to or able to change for the better, you *should* keep your kids away from them.

A few words about your relationship with your mother: In choosing a wife for yourself (and therefore a mother for your children) take a good look at your relationship with your mom because the unresolved issues you have with her will creep into your future relationships with women. Worthwhile Women are very aware of this fact. They know that a great indicator for how you will treat them down the line is to see what kind of relationship you have with your mother now. A Worthwhile Woman will steer clear of a man who can't manage to stand up to his mother when the situation arises.

Let's take an example to see how this leftover stuff with your mother can continue to be a problem for you later on with your wife. Let's say yours was that over-controlling type of mother. It doesn't really matter *why* she acted that way. Her intentions were probably good, but the effect on you was not. The fact that your father, if he was around, didn't intervene on your behalf to balance out your mom's style is another thing worth thinking about, especially in terms of how you envision being a father. For now, however, what matters is how you dealt with your bad feelings about your mother. You have to come to understand and finally make peace with what she did and how she did it or you will have too much trouble trusting other women in your life. You will read too much into what they say and do. You'll *assume* they are out to control you. Because you'll have trust problems with women, to protect yourself, you won't let yourself be known to them. Trust me: This is not good. If you don't let your partner close enough to you to really know you, you miss out on perhaps the biggest benefit of having a long-term relationship—truly feeling understood by another person who loves you. Next time February rolls around, check out the poems in the Valentine's Day cards—not the ones with dumb sex jokes but the "serious-looking" ones clearly written for the older folks. Start out with the ones that say "For my Wife" on the cover. They're a good bet to have the poems that celebrate how great it is to be with someone who truly understands you.

As I have said earlier, before you and your gal tie the knot, you should have some long talks with a person or two who knows you and your family well— someone who saw how you grew up. This person can give you some needed perspective and free you up from your past. A good therapist can help here too. Again, the money you spend in therapy will be far cheaper than a divorce. Or you can decide not to trust me on this one and go it alone. Frankly, most guys give the last answer; they keep their concerns to themselves and hope for the best. But you don't have to do that. You've slogged through this much of the book already.

There's no sense in blindly entering a marriage, let alone fatherhood. Don't be in such a hurry. Learn a little bit about her family and her relationships with *her* parents before you sign on the dotted line—and certainly before you have a baby together. A woman who has (or had) a relatively normal relationship with her parents is probably going to be an easier mate than one who did not. To be sure, there are many Worthwhile Women who had difficult and even terrible upbringings. A woman's negative childhood or background need not be a deal-breaker. The deal-breaker is how she understands her parents and makes sense of how she was raised. She doesn't have to "forgive and forget" an abusive background but she does have to understand it—and she must know how to forgive others. If not, she won't know how to build a healthy life with you. We guys aren't used to paying attention to these aspects of women. We're more focused on how they look and how they treat us while we're dating. But this is vital stuff.

4. **How much money do you think you need to have a baby?**

    a. It doesn't matter; there is never enough unless you're rich.

    b. It doesn't matter because you can adjust your lifestyle to afford a baby if you really want to be a parent.

    c. You have to have half a year's salary in the bank just in case . . .

    d. I plan to marry a rich girl.

The first three answers are okay. The problem with answer D is that if you're determined to marry a rich woman, you're not going to be worried about whether she is a Worthwhile Woman or not. You may get money from the marriage, but not much else of value. Besides which, rich people, especially those with "old money" are pretty good at protecting their cash. They have learned to spot gold diggers. If you're choosing answer D, you're a gold digger, and gold diggers of either sex have no integrity, no balls.

There is no set amount of money you need to feel secure in taking this big step to fatherhood. Answer C, a year's worth of cash in the bank, is a great idea but not reasonable for most working people. So, given the realities of your lives, you and your wife need to be clear with one another about the lifestyle you are willing to live in order to be parents. It's hard to save for a house when you have the expenses of parenthood. That car you are driving may have to last many more years than you anticipated when you bought it. Also, consider the lifestyle you are offering your kids. They tend to do best with one parent available most of the time. If one of you is going to stay home to raise kids, who is it going to be and for how long? If it's not going to be one of you, who is it going to be and what is that going to cost? How many kids are you going to have? Unlike when I was a kid in the 1960s when one income provided a pretty good living for a family, one-income families today often live pretty close to the bone. You both better be ready for the sacrifices in lifestyle or you're not going to be a happy family.

Of all the reasons why couples argue, money is right near the top of the list. Any couple that doesn't talk about how they want to manage their money *prior to getting married* is foolish and much more likely to end up divorced than the couples who go ahead and have that uncomfortable talk. Remember, the couples who are *afraid* of disagreeing end up divorced. Don't have kids without having the money-and-lifestyle conversation first. Come to some solid *mutual agreements*. You're making a mistake to plow ahead and hope your wife is going to change her mind on something that really isn't negotiable with you. The same is true for her.

5. Are you ready to think about death?

    a. Oh for crying out loud, lighten up! Babies are joyful things. Stop trying to bum everybody out.

    b. What does thinking about death have to do with becoming a parent? Are you trying to sell me life insurance?

    c. My religion has this area covered.

    d. I get it. You're warning us about how fragile life is and how something could go wrong. That sort of thing, right?

Right, that sort of thing. And no, I'm not meaning to bum everyone out. I'm also not seeing death in a particularly negative light. Sad as it is, it's an unavoidable part of life but it also brings incredible meaning to it. How often do we take on a challenge by reminding ourselves that "Life is short"? We use that fact to pump up our courage.

I've heard it said that the meaning of life is that it ends. Even if we believe in some sort of afterlife, it's clear that this lifetime ends. What we do with the time we have—and *what we pay attention to* during our turn at being alive— is up to us. You have to think about your attitude toward death because becoming a parent means bringing life into the world. It's not fair to yourself or your kids to dodge the death issue, and it's not just about buying enough life insurance. It is also about religion and spirituality and how you live life every day.

This is the last question of the test—and an unpleasant one for some people. You and your wife should *at least* have a very similar outlook on issues of life and death, religion and spirituality. First of all, there are the issues of convenience. There are the holidays to celebrate (or not). There are family traditions to continue (or not). Engaged couples often don't think these things through ahead of time and they become big, ugly issues later on. If either of you deviate from your families in terms of religion, belief, or practice, there will likely be pressure on you both, as a couple, to get back in line. This is especially true when grandchildren start to enter the picture. Religion is definitely not one of those topics that you want to put aside and assume, over time, will work out okay. If and when that pressure comes from your family or hers, you want to be on the same team. You don't want a wedge being driven between the two of you by other people over religion or anything else.

CHAPTER FOURTEEN

The Big Picture

As a Man with Balls, you will have the luxury of being tolerant of other people's differences simply because your life is not driven by fear. I'm not saying Men with Balls don't get scared, because we certainly do; we just aren't ruled by our fears. We have options when it comes to handling our fears, like seeking the advice and counsel of those we trust. This allows us to not feel threatened by people who act or believe differently—unless those actions or beliefs pose a threat to us. Men with balls judge other people by how they behave rather than how they think, believe, or who they pray to (or don't). Fear-driven cultures lack both integrity and tolerance. We say, "Live and let live." Our guiding principles are tolerance *plus safety*—the safety factor coming into play when someone's actions threaten the safety of others.

It is one thing for me to try and help you to make good choices regarding women and relationships and eventually, parenthood. That has been the goal of *Growing Balls*. We have talked quite a bit about acting with integrity, in accordance with your values. But once you get your own life in order—to your own satisfaction—you have to live and deal with the rest of us just as the rest of us have to live and deal with you. What if your values *don't* include tolerance of other people and their choices?

You've got problems, big problems, and so do the rest of us. When it comes to the lifestyles and beliefs of other people, if you can be guided by tolerance, you will be a happier, less frustrated man and you will make a better husband, father, and neighbor than a guy whose expectations of other people are rigid and controlling. Intolerant men are not happy until others behave according to their own rigid standards.

One great benefit to growing older is the gain in perspective. It's as though, from our babyhood to our deaths, our ability to *see* steadily increases. As we get more experience under our belts, most of us start to see things differently. Ask older people if their ideas, beliefs, and priorities have changed over the years, then listen to what they tell you. True, some types of people, as they age, get even more rigid in their attitudes and beliefs and less tolerant of others who disagree with them. But usually, this is not the case. What most people cannot tolerate in their younger years they more easily accept—or at least tolerate—in their later ones. This gain in perspective and tolerance is very common and directly connected to aging. There doesn't seem to be any other reason for it. It just happens. There are common folk expressions that describe the phenomenon, like "seeing things in a different light" or "getting the big picture," describing abilities that typically come with the perspective of age and maturity. Men talk about being "hard-headed" in their youth and then wising up as they get older.

So, how do older (and/or wiser) folks impart that hard-earned wisdom to the young among them to give them a head start on maturity? Traditionally, the elders teach the young ones what they have learned about life through a variety of approaches, from religious rituals to going fishing together. The teachings that are passed down during these activities come from the elders' experience of life and what has been passed down to them from previous generation. Through the trust formed in these relationships between the young and the mature, *meaning* is attached to those life experiences.

The differences between societies are found in what is taught to children.

Because all people wonder about questions of life and death, every culture must address them. We all want to feel safe in the world and we want the same for our children. We want to be able to relax during our lives; we want to let go of our worries. Unfortunately, what children learn as "the truth" about life and death often separates them from one another. In a diverse society like ours, the accompanying stress breeds intolerance.

I can best illustrate this point with a story from my childhood. It was the late 1960s and I was a Jewish kid living in a predominantly Christian community in Orange County, California. I was about nine or ten when a little Christian girl approached me on the playground. She was a sweet kid and we had a friendly relationship but we weren't particularly close friends. I remember that she looked upset when she came up to me; clearly she had been thinking about something.

"It makes me sad," she said, "that because you're Jewish you and your family are going to burn in hell when you die." This "fact" about my fate and that of my family was making it painful for her to be around me or to want me as a friend. The poor girl was really in a dilemma. Her head and her heart were clearly being torn apart over two competing truths. First, she knew, from her own experience, that *I* was a nice kid too, and not deserving of such a horrific fate. I had apparently proved myself worthy of her friendship and she liked me. Second, however, she now possessed new information. Now she *knew* something else about me, something terrible that she had never known before: I was a Jew, and because of that, "God" was condemning me and all others like me to eternal damnation.

What a horrible situation for her. She had to accept the truth of her faith in order to fit in with her family and community. But doing so meant making sense of the damnation of her little Jewish friend. Who wants to be friends with someone who is so inherently evil that he is doomed to eternal hellfire? Looking back now, I am touched that she cared enough about me to even bring up the subject.

I remember being initially speechless, but I remember how I felt. I think I managed to say something like, "Well, I don't believe that . . ." but it was an empty reply that carried no weight for her and didn't make me feel much better either. I was hurt and sad that she was being taught this horrible thing by her parents and her church. In our temple, the topic of other people's religions just didn't come up much. From what I could see, we were focused on our own beliefs. Besides which, it is kind of pointless to try and fight against such beliefs in other people. How do you talk someone out of something they were taught by their parents and their spiritual leaders? It seemed like my little friend was from another planet, and I wondered what it must be like to live in a home where your parents believed and taught such horrible things about people just because of their beliefs, not because of anything bad they might have done. Where was the tolerance in her home?

This sort of interchange, by the way, is not an uncommon experience for Jewish kids. It's just another form of prejudice. As for the little girl and me, we never talked again. There was now a wall between us that neither of us knew how to scale.

The difference between a more violent, unforgiving society and one that is much less so is the level of tolerance demonstrated by the people who live in it. This does *not* mean that everyone has to agree with one another on hot-button issues; nor do people need to share the same beliefs. Whether a relationship is person-to-person or group-to-group, tolerance only demands a policy of "live and let live," the perspective that healthy, older people come to embrace even after perhaps years of carrying one flag or another.

We all know that little kids start out tolerant of one another. Kids are pretty easygoing. The relationship I had with the little Christian girl illustrates this. Before she was taught that Jews were bad people, she had judged me according to her owns standards of friendship and had decided that I was okay. Left to their own devices, they tend to find one another's differences either irrelevant or interesting. Watch toddlers play. Their world experience is low but their ability to accept others is high. As long as one kid is not throwing sand into the face of his new playmate or stealing his toy, things are generally cool in the sandbox. To kids, it's how you *act* that counts. They don't ask nor really care how or what other kids believe. They have to be *taught* to fear, hate, or pity other people for any other reason other than how they behave. Unfortunately, that's exactly what adults often do to their children.

So, if we start our lives being tolerant and usually end up the same way, what is happening to our attitudes and beliefs in between? Simply put, we experience the unpredictability of life—which is the natural condition of all living things—and we get scared. To handle those fears and provide comfort, every culture comes up with spiritual systems and beliefs. There are essentially two kinds of systems. First, there are the "If, then" religions whose rule and myth-oriented systems offer promises of safety regarding the afterlife. This is comforting, to be sure, but followers pay a price in terms of the head/heart split that occurs when you try to know the unknowable. This head/heart split leads to a gnawing insecurity about one's own beliefs and a raging intolerance of the beliefs of others. That gnawing insecurity, that anxiety, can lead some people to act very crazy. How many times have you read that by the time the police finally catch the crazed killer or child molester, he turns out to be known as a very religious guy?

In "If-then" religions, a reward in the afterlife is possible, sure; but it's not easy and far from a done deal. There are many rules to obey; all based on opinions of what is right and what is wrong. It is "black-and-white thinking" where there's not much room for shades of gray, the "maybe-so's" of human wondering. However, you break the rules and the price you pay for your disobedience is your eternal soul. This is a very heavy burden, don't you think? The more "black and white" your thinking is, the more intolerant you become of other people who think your burden is not just wrong, but unnecessary as well. That intolerance can quickly turn into violence—man to man or society to society.

The second kind of spiritual system *allows* for more of a live-and-let-live attitude. These systems are built on observations of the natural world, and focus their followers on the task of finding their rightful place in it through personal experience. These systems encourage spiritual practice (like ways to observe the world, study, various types of meditation, and so on). They don't come with many promises. The comfort they give comes from putting their followers' lives (and eventual deaths) into the context of the natural and observable world where people are in the same category as all the other forms of life. What happens to our "soul" or "spirit" after our death may not be knowable in these systems of belief, but they point out that we're all in this life-drama together, moving through time that does not stop for anyone—so maybe there's comfort in that. From this point of view, we have much more in common with each other than we have meaningful differences. These systems believe life is to be appreciated and celebrated, and best of all, this way of thinking promotes tolerance.

Both kinds of spiritual systems use stories to illustrate their beliefs. It is the stories we use to explain the unexplainable that separate us. *The differences between societies are found in what is taught to children.*

So take a look at the spiritual system in which you were raised. Try allowing yourself to judge your religion by whether or not it allows you to be tolerant of other people and how they live their lives. Like the kid in the sandbox, you are entitled to judge another person by his or her behavior toward you and society in general. Use public safety as your bottom line. Beyond that, consider finding yourself another spiritual system to follow if the one you were raised with teaches you to be intolerant. Your head and heart need not be split apart for you to have spirituality in your life.

It is interesting that when young people (and children) are sick and dying, they often are said to teach everyone around them huge life lessons, especially in terms of acceptance of others and having a healthy perspective on life. Maybe it is because they share with older people an intimacy with their impending deaths that they are able to prioritize their (limited) energies and focus on what is important in life. The people around them often recognize the early maturity in these young people, and seizing the opportunity, learn from their sobering experience of unfairly having to face death at an early age.

Sometimes, in order for the grieving to find meaning in the death of their beloved young one, it is said that perhaps the meaning and purpose of that death was to teach these important lessons to those left behind. Maybe that's true. Maybe there are such things as souls and maybe those souls choose to live certain kinds of lives before they are born into them. I don't know. But true or not, why wait for old age or a child's fatal illness (or your own) to give you the wider perspective you need to become tolerant and mature? Who says you can't start examining your life and values now as a healthy young man? Why not learn to be tolerant now? Kids (both healthy and sick) and old people have much to teach us if we'll only listen.

The funny thing is that, if you do a better job raising your kids than your parents did raising you, your child will mature faster than you did. That would be a cause for celebration, wouldn't it? Parenting is your opportunity to raise your own teacher.

*   *   *

We older guys miss the energy we had in our teens and twenties. If we envy you younger guys about anything, it is your almost boundless energy level. As a young man, you're in your prime. Enjoy it. Appreciate it. Decide what's really important to you and then do it. You have the energy to do it *intensely*. For that matter, do *lots* of things. This is skill-building time and it is a shame to waste your time and energy on an issue of intolerance. Widen your perspective and see for yourself what your real choices are. Intolerance should be reserved for *preserving* life, not judging it. It is right to be intolerable of unjust or unsafe behaviors in other people. It is a waste of your precious time and energy to be intolerant of someone else's beliefs. If you really feel so intolerant of someone else's beliefs, you probably aren't so secure in your own.

It takes **big balls** to face the world and all it's uncertainties without the safety net of promises and absolute black-and-white answers to life's unknowable questions. And while it may be scary to leave that safety net behind, you may find it is a big relief to have your head and heart back together on the same team.

Finally, a quick thought on perspective: When I was a therapist working in a group home, I would always debrief the boys who had punched walls when they got angry. When I thought they were calm enough to listen, I would say, "You know, if you keep smashing those hands of yours into walls, when you get older you're not going to be able to do much of anything with them." My hope in saying that was to show the kid at least a snapshot of perspective: How he feels now is different from how he may feel in the future. Maybe he'd come up with a less destructive way of expressing himself.

The boys always had good reasons for wanting to punch walls. They were away from their families. This was always painful for them, even when they had been mistreated at home. The group home staff and I couldn't change their pasts. We could only keep them safe for now; and if they came to trust us a little, maybe we could also help them cope with the leftover emotional baggage from those bad experiences. In the best cases, we helped them to leave some of that baggage behind and turn those old wounds and insults into life lessons that left them stronger and better prepared for their futures. When we could plant the idea in their heads that things might get better later on—in which case having a healthy set of hands might be, well, handy someday— that's when we were doing a good job.

Like the group-home boys, we all have our pasts to understand and futures to plan. The wider our vision, the more opportunities we will see. Save your energy for making your life a good one, and do what you can to help others do the same. The world will be a better place for you and your kids.

EPILOGUE

When it comes to addressing your behavior, *Growing Balls* has set the bar pretty high. We both know it's more exciting to drive too fast or act irresponsibly or shoot off your mouth to annoying authority figures when you feel like it or (more fun yet) think with your dick than it is to follow the more responsible path laid out for you here as a young, maturing man. We both also know that even if you take this book seriously, you'll probably do some of that dumb stuff anyhow, if for no other reason than to learn the truth for yourself. I'm hoping you won't feel the need to do much of it, however, given the potentially horrible results of a bad decision mixed with some bad luck. As you get older and are faced with challenging situations, you may find it helpful to refer back to some of these chapters for ideas and guidance. The tests you have read through will certainly make more sense as you get older and/or closer to making the move toward being a husband and parent, so consider keeping the book on a nearby shelf.

After early drafts of *Growing Balls* made the rounds of my friends—the same guys whose thoughts helped inspire this book (as well as a few wonderful Worthwhile Women, including my wife, who helped shape it)—some of them asked me a pair of painful questions: (1) Are young men today willing to read about, let alone think through, the topics in *Growing Balls?* and (2) Does the book set the bar *too* high for them? (I had actually asked myself these same questions too and had foolishly hoped they wouldn't occur to anyone else.) From the start, I have had to put aside the first question, essentially: "Will young men even read this?" (if not, why bother writing directly to you guys at all?), and focus instead on the second question: "Does *Growing Balls* set the bar too high for young men today?"

The first question deserves a few comments. We adults tend to underestimate you guys when it comes to your ability to think. As a therapist who has worked with young men for over twenty years, I know young guys can think through heavy issues. True, you may not tend to read the standard, popular self-help books, but consider this: How many of them are written directly *to* you instead of *about* you? No guy wants to read about himself like he's a lab rat.

If adults will take the time to talk with (instead of to) young men, they will find that guys have plenty of thoughts and feelings; if they trust you, they will open up and tell you about them. It has certainly worked for me, even when I am not in my professional therapist role. So, if some of those talking skills have translated themselves onto paper, I can hope for some young men like you as readers.

On the other hand, if the readers of *Growing Balls* end up being mostly women and mature men, well, that could work out fine too. The real potential of *Growing Balls* for being helpful—both to individuals and to society—is its ability to start conversations. As adults, we *need* to talk about the topics in this book, both among ourselves *and* with young people, because these are the growing-up issues facing young men (and women) today. Agree, disagree: It doesn't matter. I say (as you kids do), "It's all good." As someone who has participated in many (sometimes heated) discussions about this material, I can outright *guarantee* you that *Growing Balls* can start some lively conversations for you. The chapter headings alone should do the trick.

All kidding aside, I have *never* left one of these conversations without learning something useful. Conversations, even angry ones, bring out ideas and create possibilities. So if it *is* mostly the older adults who read this book, great. I need them to step up and pay attention to the younger guys around them. I need these guys to start those conversations. The mature men need to begin mentoring the young guys who *should* read this book, but for whatever reason, won't.

By setting the bar maybe just a little higher than you can jump on your own, I am challenging mature men to step up and help out you guys who are, after all, the next generation of husbands, fathers, and social leaders. My goal in writing *Growing Balls* was to support you as you mature into manhood (and to inspire other men to support you, as well) but a book is only words and ideas on paper. What is needed now is *action*. There are plenty of Men with Balls in your community, men with wisdom and time to share, but most of them need to be asked. They won't necessarily seek you out or offer you advice. The ones who do—the teachers, program volunteers, neighbors, family friends, and relatives—these guys all deserve our appreciation.

For your part, you can't be afraid to ask for help. You can't let your pride get in the way of tapping the advice and resources of older, wiser men. It is typical of guys to try and figure things out for themselves, and often, that is a good thing.

But when it comes to all the issues of maturing into manhood, like deciding when and with whom to have sex, when and to whom to get engaged or have children and how, or if to use alcohol or drugs, going it alone is something you only do if you have no other choice. It takes balls to ask for help. So ask.

As for my female readers, the benefits to you of reading *Growing Balls* by now should be obvious, especially for the young women entering into relationships with young guys and for the single mothers out there raising their sons alone, doing their best without the help of mature men. I hope the book has pointed out that we guys are actually more complicated than women like to think we are. Sure, we love food, sports, and sex, but there is much more to us than that.

Now for the second question: If the expectations in this book don't seem altogether realistic for many guys today, why set the bar so high anyway? Two reasons: The first reason concerns you, big guy, and the second is about the rest of us because we are affected by nearly everything you do. Let's start with the first:

The overall bull's-eye of moral integrity is "Doing the right thing because it is the right thing to do." This is what motivates Men with Balls. However, at this stage of your life, if you are making the "right decisions" just to steer clear of trouble, that's fine. You're still clearing the high bar. You'll soon find, if you haven't already, that your good decisions really do leave you with more options than will your bad ones. As you mature over time, you will hopefully find satisfaction in leading a life based on that bull's-eye of integrity. The prize is a fine set of balls, the respect of your family and community, and most importantly, your own self-respect.

The second reason for setting the expectations bar high is more selfish. It is about protecting the rest of us who live with you. Every time you make a good decision regarding your personal or social behavior, there is a positive ripple effect on society. Every time you handle stress, desire, or pressure in a healthy way, you make life better not only for yourself but also for the rest of us.

I'm not exaggerating. Imagine a bored and broke fifteen-year-old with his sights set on the best and newest fifty-dollar video game. He's determined to get the game, that's for sure. The only question is how he's going to get it. If someone doesn't just give him the money, he has three clear options to scraping together the fifty dollars: He can earn, borrow, or steal it. As I write this, there are real guys in real neighborhoods facing just this kind of choice and they are on the verge of deciding just which road to take to get that game. Tomorrow, their families, neighbors, and communities are either going to reap the benefits of a good choice or pay the price of a bad one. What is it going to take for the guy to make the good decision?

Some guys will do the right thing—earning and saving their money to buy the game—not so much because that is the right thing to do but because that is what is expected of them by their families, or because they aren't willing to risk getting into trouble. As far as society is concerned, that kind of motivation is good enough. The money is earned, not stolen; the kid feels good about himself; and the game store makes a sale. No one gets cheated, hurt, or arrested. No one ends up at Juvenile Hall. No family is humiliated by having to go to court with their son. This is great, right?

But *Growing Balls* is setting the bar even higher. Doing what you are *expected* to do, or fear of getting into trouble may keep you on the straight and narrow but it hardly makes you ready to be a husband or father. For many guys, I believe it takes a mentor to inspire doing the right thing just because it is the right thing to do.

Here's another example: Right now there are young men in their twenties (and older) trying to "score" with love-struck or baby-obsessed teenaged girls. These girls are easy to spot and easy to bed, and a high percentage of them, young and fertile as they are, will get pregnant and decide to have their babies. Then what do you have? Children having children. Most of these older guys will respond to the big news by ditching the young girls *and* their unborn children *and* all the responsibilities to follow. Why? We've established that already. All they wanted was sex, not a relationship or fatherhood, and once there is a surprise baby on the way, it is easier to cut and run than to stay and do the right thing, which in this case would mean taking responsibility for your actions by dealing honestly with their consequences. Without enough pride and self-confidence to pursue mature Worthwhile Women, these immature guys go after girls who think an older boyfriend and a baby is their ticket to happiness.

Who picks up the pieces from the bad decisions? We do; you and me and the rest of the tax-paying society, we all pay the price. We pay for the all the needed social services and assistance; we pay for all the health care and counseling. And if these fatherless kids get into trouble later on, we'll end up paying pay for that too. Some of us will be the victims of their crimes, and all of us will foot the bill for their anger and misbehavior.

Remember: All kids deserve the dedicated attention of *two* mature parents who are committed to raising their children well. But many of these little ones, the ones with teenaged mothers and no fathers, don't get the support they need. Instead, for these kids to get a healthy start on life, other people have to step up to the plate and put in the time, money, and energy to help them have a good childhood. But that usually doesn't happen. Instead, the children-having-children cycle simply repeats itself, generation after generation, as the new crop of kids makes the same bad choices as did their parents. Understand that I come to these issues from the perspective of a family therapist with years of social work experience under my belt. My colleagues and I would *really* like to see this cycle end.

*   *   *

In his 1961 inaugural speech, President John F. Kennedy announced that "the torch (of leadership) has been passed to a new generation of Americans." Pointing out that his generation had been tempered by world war, he went on to ask something of young Americans that has not been asked of them since: Unbridled unselfishness. Born in the heart of the depression, Kennedy's generation grew up to be faced with a world order coming apart at the seams. In response, rich and poor men alike fought side by side, sharing the belief in *doing the right thing because it is the right thing to do.*

With the directive: "Ask not what your country can do for you; ask what you can do for you country," Kennedy set the bar high for the generation soon to follow his own. That generation was my own, the so-called Baby Boomers, who also responded with integrity: thousands of young men and women answered his call to public service in the newly formed Peace Corps.

Born in January of 1958, I was three years old when Kennedy gave that speech and too young to directly answer his call to action. My peers and I are at the tail of Baby Boomer dog. Now, however, some forty-five years later, the world is being run by those out in front, at the head of the dog. But keep this in mind: we're right around the corner from retiring, so, heads up! The leadership torch is headed your way and fast. We Boomers will have a long and impressive list of accomplishments and failures by the time we are finished at the top—that's true of every generation and will be true of yours too. But we're leaving you a messy world needing to be cleaned up, and a sick planet needing healing. So by the time your generation is ready to hand that torch to the next, you will hopefully have fewer failures and far more successes than we Boomers have managed to achieve. For you to do better than my generation has done will require the Kennedy-like inspiration of mature men and women pushing young people, guys and girls alike, to get active in positive skill-building activities. To make you a positive force in the society you are so soon to inherit, you need to achieve balance in mind, body, and spirit. The moral message over all your effort—the ethical bull's-eye—must be your belief in doing the right thing *because it is the right thing to do.* Period.

Guys, I'm sorry we adults have screwed things up for you. I'm sorry we haven't given you a better organized society to inherit. It's not fair, but we know life isn't fair anyway so you're going to have to learn to cope with the mess we are handing you—one guy at a time, one decision at a time. Meanwhile, here's this little book for you. I know you've been out there on your own, doing the best you know how to do. I respect that *and* I believe you can do better. *Growing Balls* is a reach-out from the limited but well-meaning perspective of a man in his forties, and a few of his friends, who have learned most of these lessons and grown our balls—often the hard way.

I'm just a hair short of *begging* you to stay away from marriage and fatherhood until you're ready to do the jobs right; of *begging* you to get to know yourself honestly, from the inside out; of *begging* you to think with the head on your shoulders and not the one in your pants; of *begging* you to focus on building your skills, doing things that make you proud of yourself; of *begging* you to become an expert at something so you can feel proud of yourself; of *begging* you to develop the discipline you will need to face the inevitable challenges you'll face through the years of your adult life; of *begging* you to be a real friend to your buddies.

Maybe you're one of the lucky ones who has mature men looking out for your best interests and who have worked to get you ushered into manhood. If you were not blessed with such men in your life, it's time to seek them out. When that leadership torch gets passed to your generation, society will need good strong men (and women) ready to carry it. We will need Leaders with Balls who are willing and able to really take the moral high road; leaders who will do the right thing because it is the right thing to do. We will need leaders who see the *futility* in making Wealth, Youth, and Beauty the holy trinity of moral values that they have become in our country. The Baby Boomers, despite a bright and heated start, have not managed to pull this off.

During the 1960s and 1970s, in response to a number of unfair and outdated social structures that oppressed women, dragged us into fruitless wars, and limited the possibilities of the human spirit, a group of our older Boomers experimented and explored different possibilities of living in a variety of social and personal arenas. It was a loud, splashy, and colorful bus trip that affected everyone and everything that encountered it. Admittedly, not everyone who rode that bus survived. But those who did had the honor of participating in many important personal and social conversations that resulted in some significant social progress.

But many of those possibilities the Boomers pointed to or experimented with didn't pan out. They tried to hold the country accountable for its stated values, but ideals often lost out to politics. Equal opportunity for everyone remains a nice idea, but it is not a reality. After a little initial bruising, greed stood back up and reestablished itself in the 1980s. The prevailing social attitude became that the 1960s dreams were just that—dreams—and people were well advised to get going to hurry up and claim their share of the pie no matter what it took or who got in their way. Today, the rich keep getting richer and the poor keep getting poorer.

This greedy and selfish backlash of "me getting mine"—the chase after wealth, youth, and beauty—has been winning ever since, and my friends and I are *not* happy about it. As a young man, you, like the rest of us, have been hypnotized to chase these empty and fleeting values. Now the world needs *your generation* to wake up and smell the coffee. We've been wandering this soul-less desert for forty years now. Break free of this craziness we have given to you and lead us all to a healthier place. Who knows? Maybe you are one of the leaders we're looking for.

ACKNOWLEDGMENTS

Growing Balls was sparked by a conversation with Richard Talavera on a car-ride between Grass Valley and Davis, California in the summer of 2000. It came together as a result of many conversations held since (and remembered from the past) with a wide group of wonderful men (with Balls) and Worthwhile Women. In no particular order, they are: Bill Reagan, Moses Schimmel, Rabbi Bob Bergman, Bob Zang, Eric and Ann Hafter, Larry Berent, Arnie and Enid Weinthal, Louis "Bernie" Horwitz, Dr. Dave Dycaico, the Davis Garage Group (Dan, Marty, Jacques, Ralph, Stu, Meir, Dave and Mike), Dr. Jim Conley, Dr. Austin Hurst, Dr. Joyce Welcher, David Ben-Veniste, Dr. Jeff Sugar, Master Moon, Douglas Selva, Greg Boales, Cedric Anderson, Joe Saah, MFT, Dr. Bob Oliver, Pierre "Pens" Pobre, Jeff Brewer, Mark Long, Richard Kish, Jeff Presement, Dan Meisenhoelder, Todd Hargis, Dr. Greg Orton, John Onda and Vic and John from ITU.

Thanks are due to my wife, Pam Delaney, MFT, for providing much well-reasoned and valuable content and copy editing as well as astute intellectual challenges. I am greatly indebted to my friend and colleague, Ce Eshelman, MFT, for her line-by-line critique of an early draft of *Growing Balls*. Her deft blend of support, encouragement, sarcasm and occasional outrage was instrumental in bringing this book to fruition. I am grateful as well to Arlie McDaniel, MFT, the first person to lay eyes on the early chapters, for his enthusiasm and encouragement. I kept an early email from Arlie on the wall next to my computer and it kept me going through several subsequent drafts.

James Marcus, as creative a man as I have ever known, has patiently read and given feedback on every manuscript I have ever written. He has many fingerprints on this book. Also providing early, substantive and valuable feedback and support was Doug Scott, PhD and Debi Scott, MA, Rebecca Weikle, MFT, Bill Panek, MD, Ann Panek (who actually found it useful enough to insist on purchasing a copy of an early draft), my mother, Shirley Hafter, MFT, the guys in the Garage Group, my sister, Tonia Hafter and Dr. Jeffery Smith: All had a hand in shaping the final outcome. The support from my father, Lawrence Hafter, is forever appreciated as was the lesson he taught me early on: "Do the right thing because it is the right thing to do."

Made in the USA
San Bernardino, CA
16 March 2017